EXACTING CLAM No. 1 — Summer 2021

CONTENTS

Front cover: "Chowder Laps" by Kathleen Nicholls

Interior drawings by Kathleen Nicholls, John Patrick Higgins, & Jacob Smullyan

© 2021 Sagging Meniscus Press
All Rights Reserved

ISBN: 978-1-952386-18-3

Exacting Clam, the Discerning Mollusk's Guide to Arts and Ideas, is a quarterly publication from Sagging Meniscus.

Senior Editors: Aaron Anstett, Jesi Bender, Jeff Chon, Elizabeth Cooperman, Tyler C. Gore, Charles Holdefer, Kurt Luchs, M.J. Nicholls, Doug Nufer, Thomas Walton

Executive Editor: Guillermo Stitch

Publisher: Jacob Smullyan

exactingclam.com

Steven Moore

Taking It Personally

Introduction to Greg Gerke's
See What I See (2nd ed.)
Zerogram Press, April 2021

Greg Gerke's *See What I See* is a splendid example of the return of the personal in modern literary criticism. Up until World War II, a reader could often sense a flesh-and-blood person behind literary critiques, but upon the arrival of bloodless New Criticism, such writing became more impersonal, and under the influence of the continental criticism of the 1960s it took on a quasi-scientific tone. As the hermeneutics of suspicion took hold of them, critics distanced themselves from the works they interrogated, and it became hard to tell if they even liked literature. Writing in 1892 of the heroine of Swift's novella *Polite Conversation*, the great George Saintsbury confessed, "I fell in love with her when I was about seventeen, I think; and from that day to this I have never wavered for one minute in my affection for her." Can you imagine a professional critic writing that today about a fictional character? (And make no mistake: Saintsbury is a greater critic than any academic writing today.) Unabashed enthusiasm for a book or a character became the sign of an amateur: a member of a neighborhood book club, or a reviewer on Amazon.

On two occasions Gerke quotes T. S. Eliot's famous line, "The progress of an artist is a continual self-sacrifice, a continual extinction of personality." But I don't think that's always true of artists; if you knew nothing about Eliot's life, you could pretty accurately guess from his poetry what kind of personality he had, a totally different one from that which emerges from the poems of his free-spirited contemporary E. E. Cummings. Critics, on the other hand, have indeed pursued "the extinction of personality," even down to the strict avoidance of the first-person "I." In Gerke's case, on the other hand, the personal approach is apparent even in his title: *See What I See*, not what an impersonal "one" sees.

In recent years, however, some critics have woven their personal involvement with a novel into their critiques; I'm thinking of Michael Gorra's *Portrait of a Novel: Henry James and the Making of an American Masterpiece* (2012), Maureen Corrigan's *So We Read On: How The Great Gatsby Came to Be and Why It Endures* (2014), and Rebecca Mead's *The Road to Middlemarch: My Life with George Eliot* (2014), each of which gave me a greater appreciation for those novels than any academic treatises on them. No difficulty here trying to decide if the critics liked the novels they wrote about, nor did their enthusiasm muzzle any misgivings they may have had about any shortcomings.

See What I See is a welcome addition to this trend. This collection puts into practice William H. Gass's belief that "Works of art are meant to be lived with and loved." In prose as beautiful and imagistic as Gass's, Gerke recounts how he has lived with and loved certain authors and filmmakers. Especially in his discussion of books he often mentions the circumstances in which he read a particular author, the binding of the book and font, even the time of day: "Is late afternoon the best time for poetry? With a sinking sun and the stories of our lives in repose after the often fitful midday, aren't the siesta hours most befitting an artform so benighted by dreams, the sleep of dreams, and dreamlike imagery?" He likes the smell of certain books, is aroused by what he calls (in "Holy Hill") the "eros of language," and dotes on the sensuality of reading. After quoting the opening paragraph of John Hawkes's *Blood Oranges*, he writes "The passage presses its sweet side to the reader," as if the prose had metamorphosed into an armful of warm girl. He gets horny at times, trying to decide if he should "[h]op into bed with [Elizabeth] Bishop or Borges?" and wonders if he should add Henry James's *Italian Hours* to his "discriminating list of books to shag." In the same randy essay ("How to Live, What to Read") we catch him "stroking the spines of a few new books I've just bought . . . clothed or naked."

William H. Gass, it quickly appears, is the tutelary genius presiding over the literary half of this collection. (The book is divided into essays on literature and on film, with an intermezzo on "Real Life.") He's one of the dedicatees of the book, and while not named in the first essay is alluded to twice. ("Art has taken precedence. I've fallen deeply into it and can barely return to life" is adapted from *Willie Masters' Lonesome Wife*, and "Life in a chair . . ." is from *The Tunnel*.) There are two essays on Gass, and he is often cited in the other essays in the first half of the book. What Gerke loves most about Gass is his attention to sentences; Gass wrote several essays about sentences, and titled one of his collections *Life Sentences*, for he felt the main goal of a literary work was to offer as many beautifully crafted sentences as possible. Gerke echoes this belief as he writes of "the music of sentences," of "that gargantuan or miniature unit called the sentence." He praises Henry James's "architectonic sentences," his "singular syntactical sensations," and claims "The beauty of James' sentences victimizes us." Following in the footsteps of these masters, Gerke offers a steady stream of beautiful sentences of his own, rich in imagery. Of his fellow subway riders, he writes: "They nodded off, punched at or swiped the screens of their phones as if scraping frosting from a cooling cake. An older women, with the hard angles of an Eastern European face and short hair colored by a box of chestnut dye, sat hunched with a heavy book." Not an upscale bottle or tube of dye but a "box," and note the alliteration of "hard . . . hair . . . hunched . . . heavy"—perhaps an homage to the *h*-

alliterations he had noted earlier in Wallace Stevens's "A Rabbit As King of the Ghosts."

In addition to Stevens—the subject of two appreciative essays and lovingly cited elsewhere—another tutelary genius of this book is Gass's friend William Gaddis, who is mentioned throughout, beginning on the first page. He is the subject of three essays: one on *Carpenter's Gothic*, another on *A Frolic of His Own*, and a review of Joseph Tabbi's 2015 biography. Even in these critical assessments, the personal touch presides: I've read virtually everything written about Gaddis, but never an essay that begins, "There are stolen moments when raising a young child, the let-up during nap-time being a prime example. In one of these recent pauses, I read to my wife the beginning of the fifth chapter or section (they are unnumbered) of William Gaddis's 1985 novel *Carpenter's Gothic*. . . ." In the one on *A Frolic of His Own*, Gerke explains that he read Gaddis's legal novel concurrently with his wife, a criminal defense attorney, and adds anecdotes of his own involvement in the legal profession. Gerke reminds us that novels are read in the real world—he often reads on the subway—by real people with real jobs, which is rarely conveyed, or is considered irrelevant, in academic criticism.

The other recipients of Gerke's loving attention include Rainer Maria Rilke, Louise Glück, Gertrude Stein, Geoffrey Hill, Patrick White, Don DeLillo, and V. S. Naipaul. The final essay in the first half is entitled "Why Write?," which is not merely an academic question. In addition to essays, Gerke writes fiction too—he has two short-story collections to his name, *There's Something Wrong with Sven* (2009) and *Especially the Bad Things* (2019), with a lengthy novel in the works—which accounts for his sensitivity to the fiction of others. As I've written elsewhere, I've always felt that novelists often make better critics than academics for the obvious reason that they know what it's like to actually write a novel: they've struggled with conceiving and developing an idea, finding a form, breathing life into characters, plotting the narrative, revising and aestheticizing their work, and finally seeing it through the press, sometimes even defending it from doubtful editors. They've walked the walk, and consequently are far more qualified to talk the talk than professors or book-reviewers who have never tried their hand at fiction, and thus have only a theoretical notion of what goes into writing it. Gerke concurs in one of the last essays in this book: "Critics carry the stain of envy into the thoughts they print, especially those emboldened enough to critique without having ever made the art that can exasperate them."

The personal takes center stage in the four auto-biographical essays in the "Real Life" intermezzo, all engaging, masterfully written, and marbled with references to books and films. Then he shares the stage with several auteur directors for the final section, "The Silver Screen." Gerke confesses in the book's opening essay that filmmaking was his "first passion" as teenager, and in a later essay on director Paul Thomas Anderson he tells us that he attended film school for two years before leaving with "numerous Bergman-enamored screenplays that would never see production." He turned to writing instead, switch-hitting thereafter between fiction and nonfiction. I am not a cinephile and haven't seen many of the movies he analyses, or even heard of some of the directors—is Maren Ade a real name or a playful pseudonym?—but this half of the book strikes me as just as intelligent and well-written as the first half, and if anything is even more personal.

As with the literary essays, the focus is on the roles his favorite films have played in his life, privileging subjective over objective analysis. As Gass said, "Works of art are meant to be lived with," and in the section's opening essay on Michelangelo Antonioni—whose *Blow-Up* is one of my all-time favorite movies—Gerke gives us a perfect example of that sentiment: "I have to admit there is something about Antonioni that is deeply embedded in my soul, and though the psychical manifestation of his art is a little riven by time, its granite face can still proudly display a freckling of mica by my own sun. It is a force that surely resists many people, and though I believe I've grown out of taking up a cause to rebuke those I would label impoverished, I only extol to eradicate my own glowering, to teach myself the lesson of how as I get older, much of his work only gets better." The Italian director would agree with this approach, for Gerke quotes him as saying, "That is why the best way to watch a film is to have it become a personal experience. At the moment in which we watch a film, we unconsciously evoke what is inside of us, our life, our joys and our pains, our thoughts—our 'mental vision of the past and the present,' as Susan Sontag would say." Similarly, in his essay on Stanley Kubrick's longest film, Gerke asks, "What makes *Barry Lyndon* my own story? Have I lived to subsume it or have I subsumed it to live?" Sometimes a work of art will tell him "You must change your life"—he quotes the famous last line of Rilke's "Archaic Torso of Apollo" near the end—and other times he skewers films that can't be lived with, crass Hollywood productions like *The Social Network* and *Drive* that "drain me of my life spirit."

Although he can intellectually analyze a film with the best of them, Gerke has a physical reaction to his favorites: in his essay on Ingmar Bergman—who, along with Éric Rohmer, plays the same role of tutelary genius for film as Gass does for literature—he writes, "I can always tell how good a film is if my armpits smell afterward. The body doesn't lie." All of his film essays convey nuts-and-bolts information about his chosen directors, but any film critic could do that; Gerke mixes the informative with the confessional, and to an extent that not many film critics would dare.

In some of these essays, the personal becomes almost uncomfortably revealing. In the long essay on Rohmer, for example, he aligns the actresses in some of the French director's Moral Tales series with old girlfriends. While not neglecting technical matters, such as the shade of gray in the 35mm film stock Rohmer sometimes used, Gerke is more interested in what his films tell him about himself. "How can I see my past better in this film?" he asks, "for to come to *Claire's Knee* is to be in the company of a woman I lived with the longest until my marriage, and to dwell on that time reminds me of my greatest failings." He restates this at various times in this section, as in the opening of his essay on South Korean director Hong Sang-soo: "Isn't the miracle of art how we see the panoply of our own lives via a magical panopticon? Every time we look, we see something that's really all about us." In the wrong hands, this approach can lead to the impatient rejection of certain works of art because one "can't relate" to them. That's why he goes on to caution, "It might not be easy to see one's life in film—not in the narrative itself, but in the regard of the camera, the editing, how people say things and what their silences are like."

In the book's closing essay, in which Gerke alternates between critiquing director Mike Leigh's *Mr. Turner* and musing on the role of criticism today, he evokes "poet-critic Guy Davenport, whose essays are jewels, and who claimed to be 'not writing for scholars or critics, but for people who like to read, to look at pictures, and to know things.'" That is Gerke's audience too—though "scholars and critics" could learn a few things from his personal approach. Whether writing about film or literature, honeymooning in Paris or consuming Combos, Greg Gerke bedazzles us with his keen intelligence, wide knowledge, and stylistic flair. *See What I See* is a beguiling collection of belletristic essays meant for those of us for whom art is a passion, not a profession or a pastime but a way of life.

Marvin Cohen

Surf & Verse

AT THE OCEAN'S EDGE,
AS THE SURFERS PLY THEIR PLEDGE

The put-together words of a poem
are like waves that create foam
on the beach-head from the mighty ocean
plunging down with commotion.
Then the next wave will crash again,
and the surf-divers leave their pads,
swirling away like disrupted lads
falling apart at the seams,
or so it aquatically seems.
But the surf-divers recover
and each is ready for his lover
to wipe the brine from his bronzed body
and the sea slime from his athletic hobby.
They all meet at the restaurant lobby.

VERSE ADVERSE TO FAME
PLAYS IN FAILURE'S GAME

A failed poem in the garbage can
had ambition to be in print.
But failure of rhyme and reason
spoiled the poem's hoped-for season
in the sun for strangers' eyes
to deliver fame of ego size
to that poor mediocre poet . . .
to achieve only failure—wouldn't you
   know it?
If he had talent, why didn't he grow it?
Thus his poems one by one
sink in cruel darkness over the sun.

Paolo Pergola

Rankings

Original title: "Posizioni in classifica". Published in Italy by Babbomorto Edizioni (2018). Translated by the author.

According to Darwin, life is nothing but a competition. Therefore, being a competition, everyone would do well to set a specific ranking as their goal. Obviously, for example, many people want to come in first, again according to Darwin. If you can't come in first in the hundred meters at the Olympics, which seems to me to be the apotheosis of excelling, then it's better to look for something in which you can excel. In high school, I was the best in the "high jump with a ballpoint pen".

The "high jump with a ballpoint pen" takes place during Latin class. Put two Latin dictionaries side by side, lying with their backs facing outward, and their pages facing inward. Next, insert a pen across the pages of the two dictionaries, like a horizontal bar. To get over the bar, use a ballpoint pen. Load it by placing it at about sixty degrees, in front of the bar. Then let it go. The pen will leap into the air, and jump over the bar. To sum it up, I was the champion in this discipline, in my class. With my ballpoint pen, I managed to jump over a bar that was a full seven inches high. It took four Latin dictionaries, two on either side, to produce such a height.

❧

In the moment, I was pleased to be the best. But I soon realized that the fame derived from that record was not for me. First of all, everyone kept borrowing my magic ballpoint pen, which was wearing out from so much jumping. Plus, I felt like I had become the center of attention, which I never really liked. And it seemed like all I knew how to do was launch my pen up in the air.

I began to think that it would be better to come in second. I was inspired by Cruijff's Dutch National team, or Puskás's Hungarian one, legendary soccer teams that had come in second while being much stronger than those that had somehow come in first. The Dutch had reinvented soccer, as my father once told me, since he had seen that World Cup. Their playing style was "total soccer", everyone defending and everyone attacking. They were an unbeatable team, the game started and it looked like they had already won. This was true up until they reached the final. Then the Germans got in the way, with their German soccer made up of impediments, and they impeded the Dutch to such an extent that they won the trophy. But in everyone's mind, that World Cup was forever remembered as Holland's World Cup.

The same goes for the Hungarians. They too were the strongest of all, they had not lost a game in years, they were in a different league. They too were beaten in a final by a German team, which was not as good, my father used to tell me. It was still not clear how this could happen, but nevertheless Hungary remained a legendary team. I thought about Holland and Hungary for a while, and then one day, during a Latin class while the professor was testing one of my classmates sitting in the front, we organized yet another pen-jumping contest.

That time, I decided to let Brizzano, my desk mate, win. Both of us had jumped six-and-a-half inches. He had a brand new pen; which jumped like a bunny. However, mine was still in good condition, I was sure I could jump more than seven inches, I had already done it at home, though no one knew about it. But I was tired of coming in first, I was still thinking about Holland and Hungary, so I missed the jump. Brizzano' s pen surpassed seven-and-a-half inches and he won. I came in second.

I discovered that coming in second wasn't for me either. My teammates were making fun of me. I had been defeated. I was a loser. I fell into a kind of depression. I started coming in last in the ballpoint pen jumping competition, on purpose. We had started studying Nietzsche, and I was inspired by him, not the superman-Nietzsche, of course, but the nihilist-Nietzsche. This idea intrigued and confused me. On the one hand, Nietzsche was talking about the superman, that is, about excelling, I thought. Something that I had already discarded as a philosophy, since I had come in first in the "high jump with the ballpoint pen" and I hadn't liked it that much. On the other hand, Nietzsche was a nihilist, which to my way of thinking meant denying the values of the world. So, if people in the world wanted to excel, then to do the opposite was to lose.

As a result, I decided to lose, no matter what, and losing for me was also synonymous with coming in last, in everything I did. Hence, I began to get the lowest grades in the class in all subjects, even in Philosophy, where clearly I had not understood anything about Nietzsche. Above all, I began to come in last in the "high jump with the ballpoint pen" in which I had become a dud. However, my new, somewhat rebellious attitude, did not go unnoticed by my parents, who gave me a long speech that began with "Listen up" and ended with "bacon". Coming in last at all costs was not going to work.

While I was mulling over what to do, it turned out, during literature class, that certain writers had written not about heroes, nor about rebels or out-

casts who would come in last in the ranking. A new figure of the average man had emerged, and it suited me just fine. Translated into grades at school, it certainly meant getting a pass in all subjects. Translated into performances in the "high jump with the ballpoint pen," it meant coming in more or less in the middle. If there were twelve of us participating, that is, the boys in our class plus a couple of girls tagging along, I made sure to finish sixth or seventh.

Yet even now, after a while, I wasn't satisfied. No one noticed me anymore, which would be the aim of the average man, I thought, but it also had the side effect that the two girls who participated in the "high jump with the ballpoint pen", especially Matilde Mairoldi, the prettiest one, didn't talk to me anymore. Nothing doing. It seemed to me that I had tried everything, inspired first by Darwin, then by Holland, by Nietzsche, and finally by the average man. But none of these strategies had convinced me. I thought to myself, was there something I hadn't tried?

Third. I hadn't tried to come in third yet. Third place, that was a brilliant position to be in. I was podium worthy, but not defeated like those who came in second. I had laurels, but they were not as heavy as the winner's. Matilde Mairoldi began to talk to me. She talked to me, and I talked back. We saw each other more and more often, even outside of school. While my classmate Brizzano and one of his buddies, who always came in second, were all concentrating on practicing for the "high jump with the ballpoint pen", Matilde Mairoldi and I were discovering brand new games all on our own.

GUILLERMO STITCH

THE BLURRED, BROWNIAN BORDERS OF SUPPOSEDLY SHARP THINGS

Phelan had requested Fast Rope Insertion Extraction System, specifically. It was faster than rappelling and she was in a hurry. The chopper banked, sweeping in over the crescent of a little bay, and she ran a hand up and down her torso going through last minute checks. *Always in a hurry*, she thought, slowly stroking the coiled rope.

"One minute," said Whelan.

Most of the kit was going down first on a separate line: her rifle (an L115a4 chambered for Lapua Magnum .338's with night sights and a sound suppressor, disassembled in its case), Nolan's guns, smart phone, cash.

"Stand by."

She took up the ready-to-exit position and Whelan slapped her back.

"Go."

Leaving the aircraft and rotating her body ninety degrees, she placed the rope between the arches of her feet and dropped. About two thirds of the way down her grip tightened to slow her descent, but she hit the ground on a steep bank of earth in the darkness and had to steady herself with the braided cord, looking up as she moved away and Nolan emerged from the Apache AH 64D. In a few seconds he was with her. They took one handle of the heavy kit bag each and made

their way almost doubled over to the road. At its side there was a stream in a gully where they took up position and waited while the Apache rose to surveillance altitude.

The mark would probably be moving now, alerted by the noise. They would hang on here though—no point in trying to cover this ground on foot. Target could have been here for days getting to know the short cuts and rat runs. She was already familiar with the terrain (she knew, for instance, that they were behind the Giametti house) but it was for the most part forest and farm land: large flat fields separated by hedgerows that constituted a network of concealed ditches and water ways. A little to the south it got hilly and covered with dense scrub. There was only the one aircraft for support. Better to wait for visual.

She checked her Tresor P8686. The watch distinguished itself with its tritium-illuminated second hand which allowed her to carry out precision timings in total darkness. Tritium light is modest so there is no tell-tale glow.

"Two minutes twenty seconds," said Nolan, "and we'll have UAV."

His hand was feeling around in his Mülle compression bag and emerged holding a neat aluminium foil parcel which he proceeded to unwrap. "You have the thermos."

She ripped open the side pocket of her black c122 tacticals and pulled out the contoured carbon-fibre flask.

"Is it tea or coffee?" asked Nolan.

"Tea," she replied. "I put sugar in."

"Good. These are boiled ham." He put the sandwiches—on the little tin foil tray he had fashioned—down on the ground between them and took one.

"Who's the RP?" asked Phelan.

"Dolan," said Nolan.

She checked her watch again. "One minute thirty. What have we got? Reaper?"

"Salamander. High altitude, heat sensing. Dolan's a dab hand with it."

"We have voice?"

Nolan indicated the encrypted smart phone.

She took a sip of tea, her mouth full. "Lovely taste of butter."

Nolan nodded vigorously. "We can't risk detection on foreign soil, so we'd better get on it quickly and identify target inside a minute or two, I'd say. A vehicle we can use will be along soon."

This wasn't foreign soil for Phelan but no matter. Nolan was the details guy and she trusted him with them; it meant she could keep her eye, and her mind, on the prime.

"Forty seconds."

H e was very particular about the light, yes. Magical was the word he kept coming back to.

"It's gotta be magical!" he'd say. "Can you gimme that?"

Well of course I could. It's what I do, isn't it? Problem was I wasn't sure what he meant. He had this way with words. Bit cryptic.

"I want everything *illuminated*," he said to me this one time. "Can you do that for me, Sparky?"

Well, yes. Problem was I didn't know what he meant. So anyway, I had to come up with something, especially for the crossroad scene which was so key for him. Then it occurred to me—tritium.

A neat tie-in. We fed tubes of it through all the hedges and fastened some beneath the eaves of the house. It sort of gave everything this kind of border, you know? It separated things. Nothing so crass as standard fluorescent strips, or neon. A lot more subtle than that. Gave everything this heightened, unreal appearance. Like stadium lighting or something, but you know, subtle. I was very pleased. I think he was too. He seemed to be.

"Y our brother is gone," they'd told her when they'd gotten back to the compound.

It was the second time her world had come to an end.

The first had been the day she'd learned, as she played in the sand pit out behind the latrines, that a .300 Win Mag sniper round had entered her father's head just above his right eye and exited, along with her innocence or any shot she would ever have at a quiet life, at the back of his neck. The injury hadn't been all that easy to find, apparently, on the charred corpse. Nolan, who had been there forever, had been the one to tell her about her father with his customary attention to specifics and it was Nolan now, looking her straight in the eye with his hand on her shoulder as she knelt in the vegetable patch, telling her she didn't have a brother anymore.

"He's gone," he said, his voice controlled, "and that's it. We can feel sorry for ourselves once the job is done. It's very much down to you now, Phelan. We're utterly dependent on you."

The job. *Her* job, now.

She looked from Nolan's face to Mullen's, to Whelan's, then at the ground. The world wasn't spinning—her training had been too thorough for that—but it wanted to. A few of the breath cycles that Cullen had taught her and she was ready to ask the question.

"How?"

Nolan took his hand away and averted his eyes. He clearly didn't wish to talk about it, but he had to know that she would never let it rest. "On foot."

She bit her dirty nails. It took a couple of seconds to register. "Excuse me?"

His hand was back on her shoulder, squeezing. "Don't bite your nails. And don't worry, Phelan. He'll be fine." He was pacing a little, still withholding eye-contact. "We weren't too far from the 33A bus stop. That line runs approximately every fifteen minutes at peak times, as you know, and the Vale & Valley Bus Company has an excellent track record for punctuality. I checked—"

"Wait a second . . . sorry, I just thought you were telling me my brother was dead."

Uproarious laughter.

"No not dead, you silly bean," chortled Mullen. Then he frowned. "Just kind of . . . *deflated,* I suppose."

Whelan lit a cigarette. "Yes, there was a visible sagging wasn't there? Poor chap. I guess he just wasn't up for it anymore."

He swept his arm through an arc that took in the latrines and barracks, the Apache, the 4 x 4's, the 1942 Dodge WC-56, the 8.8cm Flak 41, the Ostwind, the Kugelblitz, the D-30 Lyagushka howitzer, the ARTEC Boxer, a pallet of AA mine dischargers and the M777 UFH, two Type 4 AA 20m machine cannons, the BTR-3, the BTR-4, the BTR-94, the Cloud Leopard, the Oshkosh, the Pindad and his own meticulously arranged row of Jatimatics.

"You know," he said from beneath the smoke halo that rose as he put the packet back in his pocket. "*This.*"

An amazing, amazing person.

So special.

Amazing.

Not a very effective communicator, in my opinion.

I've worked with the greats, as you know.

Taking instruction from him was . . . it was as if he didn't know what he wanted. What he was trying to do.

"Phelan is a hundred percent focused on her mission," he would say. "A thousand percent. What she herself refers to as the prime. It's crucial that we see that."

He'd pat each word into my back as I stepped on set.

"At the same time I would like us to get a profound sense of preoccupation from her, if we could."

At which point it was *Action!* And away I'd go . . .

I mean, what am I supposed to do with that? You tell me somebody who can do focused and preoccupied at the same time and I'll shut up.

I will shut up.

The people I've worked with.

I bluffed it, in the end. Tried to look as blank as possible throughout. Seemed to work for him. Still these are the pitfalls aren't they?

An amazing person. Truly wonderful.

Joyful experience for me, the whole thing.

Privilege.

Amazing.

Squatting on the lip of the gully. The unlit road stretching out ahead of them and behind. Whelan paying close attention to the phone, the screen illuminating his face.

"OK, we have UAV."

A moment later. "And target."

Phelan bent over the screen.

Dolan was keeping the drone trained on the crossroads. The imaging had that centrifugal near-wobble of a camera mounted on something high up and circling. She could see the football ground and the brambles.

The orange roof.

The fields behind.

A garden wall ran along one corner of the intersection. Behind it an anomalous and somehow familiar mass of brighter light.

Target.

She knew that wall. It was low. He was desperate. "He's going to bolt. This thing keep up with him when he does?"

Uproarious laughter from Nolan, and Dolan over the phone

"This is Salamander, Phelan," said Nolan, "a high altitude version of Chameleon. It's got *everything*. There isn't anything, in other words, that it doesn't have."

Fingertip to fingertip he tapped through the specs.

"Fully integrated airlectrics.

"Error-permissive triple-helix flight deck tech.

"Ultra.

"Very.

"Gps.

"It's Tcas ready.

"Ermp," said Dolan.

"Yes. This thing could hang around up there for over thirty hours if it needed to.

"It's electro-optical and infra.

"It's got INS.

"It's Ocelot SOR capable.

"And it's fully Gnu SITCOM compatible."

"OK," said Phelan. "Good."

W hen Crampton Electrivans (a part of the Hiker Siddleton group) introduced their D-range Battery Electric Urban Transport Vehicle, they were entering an arena that had been dominated for many years by that colossus of the battery powered urban transport sector—the Scotland & Harris Roadfinder. It was an audacious move but nobody could accuse Crampton of not having done their homework. Where the Roadfinder had plied its trade for years with a steel-housed hypoid reduction array on a semi-floating rear axle, the D-range boasted a triple augmented spring bevel (fully floating) and introduced optional ratios.

That had to have stung at Scotland & Harris, especially since Crampton clients could still choose hypoid reduction if they wished—an unprecedentedly customer-centred approach. And it wasn't just the rear axle. As D-ranges began showing up everywhere with their magnetic blow-outs (for rapid curve extinction), upholstered driver seats and carbon-fibre covered cabs, the Roadfinder began to look like yesterday. A design classic by all means, but a bit of a period piece—Neanderthal to the Homo Sapiens of Hiker Siddleton.

If there was one aspect of battery-powered urban transport and delivery systems that the D-range didn't revolutionize, it was speed. It's vastly improved payload capacity—at just under two thousand kilos—was a mixed blessing; the vehicle's ability to handle gradients was hampered and its top speed limited to around twenty-three kilometres per hour, barely quicker than the older Scotland & Harris.

It's failure to contribute in this area had consequences for both the D-range itself—just a few years later it was superseded by Firebird Engineering's Trailblazer, an upstart with an unheard of top speed of sixty-five kilometres per hour—and for Phelan, who had been keeping her eye on the tiny pair of headlights in the distance for a couple of minutes now. They didn't seem to be getting any closer. Without turning her head she held out a hand in Nolan's direction and waved her fingers.

"Bnocks."

Hesitantly, Nolan handed over his Leopold Mark 3 Field 10x50's. They were a high-performance pair of phase-filmed binoculars housed in a shock-absorbing gunmetal grey armour, and they had a very special feature—a rotatable mildot, optimal for ranging any object that wasn't perfectly horizontal or vertical, thus allowing the user to determine range without tilting the entire binocular. They'd come in a felt-lined, soft leather pouch. Phelan took a good long look at the lights. Keeping her eyes on the road, she handed the Leopolds back to Nolan, who wiped them.

"Quick question for you, Nolan."

"Shoot."

"Asked in the spirit of enquiry, and only that."

"Yes."

"With an open mind. It isn't a *loaded* question."

"I understand."

"It doesn't constitute criticism, is what I'm saying. I wouldn't want you to think that."

"Why would I?"

"Well it could, I suppose—the question—be taken as a challenge. The expression of a wish, on my part, to revisit a decision of yours."

"Robust exchange is fundamental to the way we work, Phelan. To the team."

"OK. Good. Well—"

"Timing is important, of course."

"Quite. OK—"

"There's no point in revisiting spilt milk, for example."

"Absolutely. And the analogy is apt."

"..."

"OK, so the question is this. Is that our vehicle?"

"Yes."

"Because it looks like a milk float, to me."

"More specifically, a Crampton D-Range Four Forty, yes."

"Oh, is it the Four Forty? A classic of course. You wouldn't have considered the VXA30, which now holds the land speed record? Or even a vamped up Mulberry? They can be quite nippy. I'm just thinking of the *pursuit* element in what we're trying to achieve here, today."

"Had to go with what was there, old chap," said Nolan, popping the Mark 3's back into their pouch. "Oh, you won't need *that*."

Phelan had drawn her Hochler & Kick MK40, a semiautomatic pistol with a 16-round magazine, sound suppressor and laser aim. Loaded with Minus-T multiwadcutter-type truncated cone cartridges, at close quarters it was her weapon of choice.

"We've had two of our own embedded with the dairy for weeks now," said Nolan, "so the float is already ours. We can just hop on."

"Logan?" asked Phelan.

"And Hogan, yes," said Nolan. "So you see as well as the pursuit thing, we do need to get everybody's milk out this morning. At least until the job is done."

The great advantage for me of course is that very few people know what I look like. I can walk right down the street. Buy a newspaper. Whatever I like. It really is marvellous. I don't read newspapers though.

It's well documented now so I don't suppose there's any need to go over it again. But briefly: I started out as a circus act. Back end of a horse amongst other things. Made a bit of name for myself as a gorilla—a lot of people at the time were totally convinced. There isn't any footage of the incident, but I've spoken of it extensively. I continue to do a lot of work for gorilla charities and I see no reason to continually apologise.

My big break was the hugely successful Larry Labrador franchise for Silver Screen Studios. A modern classic. My motion capture performance was the obvious solution—if you aren't going to go down the traditional animation route—to that age old cinematic problem: the talking dog. It was actually very emotional for me because I was channeling a childhood pet. The critics have been very kind. Absolutely marvellous, in fact.

Performing as a turd, or a stool or whatever you want to call it, presented me with a whole new set of challenges. A lot of actors wouldn't have gone anywhere near this. Post-evacuation, it is of course an inanimate object, but that isn't why I was brought in. My brief was to bring the colonic, pre-evacuation stage to life—the squeezing, slipping motion, with some bending.

I was very fortunate to be invited along to the Royal Institute of Colonoscopy to research the role. Marvellous people there and the agility of your average lower intestine is simply astounding, I can tell you. I could see at that stage that I'd have my work cut out for me. The other change of course was the costume. I'd done nothing but motion capture for some years so it was a surprise. Very old-school. He had his reasons though.

"It's the texture, Brett. The glisten. We can't animate that."

You know those Japanese lanterns? Made of paper, pulled over wire rings? Well that was it. Very basic, very arts and crafts. I could be topped and tailed to free my head and feet—you know, so I could get around the set and have lunch and so on.

He was such a stickler. They tried all sorts of things to get it right and finally settled on the obvious—melted chocolate. Milk and dark, to create a realistic variegation across the surface, and they did a good job with wooden spoons, creating ripples and fissures to mimic the lines of compaction on a real stool.

He finally got his glisten with a honey-water mix. Another obvious choice but then we so often overlook the obvious, don't we? Anyway, they got there in the end. I imagine it's some kind of mucus, in reality? But honey and water did the trick.

I personally think it's where a lot of the onscreen magic comes from. That contradiction. I was a jarring presence on the set, I can tell you. Visually repugnant, of course, but at the same time delightful to the senses of smell, taste and touch. It must have been quite something to watch the make-up crew as they applied the coating.

And while it might be fanciful of me, I think you can see that frisson in the final cut; the crew would line up outside the rubber tubing we used for the intestine—they would squeeze at rhythmic intervals to propel me toward the anal ring, which they'd made out of an old inner tyre, and I really do believe that ambivalence comes across. I smelled fabulous! The whole set-up really walked that line between allure and disgust, you know?

Of course you wouldn't have the visual element in a real colon—it would be very dark in there.

The float was close. It had come to a stop outside the Giametti house and a little light flicked the cab interior into view. Hogan and Logan were bent over a piece of paper which Hogan was holding up against the dashboard. Logan ran his finger up and down the page and Hogan followed intently. There was an exchange—an unhappy one of whisperbarks, out of place in the quiet of nearnight.

Logan stabbed the page with his finger. Hogan shook his head. He pulled the page from the dashboard and out of Logan's grasp. Logan stepped out of the cab and lit a cigarette.

"What's the matter with them?" asked Phelan.

"Come on," said Nolan.

They took a handle each and covered the few metres to the little milk truck quickly.

"Hogan," said Phelan.

"Phelan," said Hogan.

"Nolan," said Logan.

"Logan," said Nolan.

"Hogan," said Nolan.

"Nolan."

"Is that everybody?" asked Nolan

"No," said Phelan, "I haven't said hello to Logan."

"Hello Phelan," said Logan.

"Hello."

"Everything OK here, chaps?" asked Nolan.

"It's him," said Hogan. "He's taken it down wrong."

"I took down what you told me to," said Logan. "You wouldn't let me have the phone."

"Come off it. You know what you're like."

"There's no harm done. I'll leave a note."

Logan's voice was becoming a little shrill. Nolan looked nervously to the Giametti house.

"It isn't as if we have a choice," said Hogan.

The crates of milk had been stacked high and arranged around a cavity where Phelan and Nolan could conceal themselves. They threw the bag into the space and followed it in. When Logan got back from the Giametti's front door, they set off.

I t was a mint morning of red cheeks and breath puffs. Dry teeth and a clear day emerging from the murk. The day world. Some of the households—the earliest risers—would be cranking up. Lights on, socks on, toast made, fires lit. Low stripe of bright on the eye-level horizon. The wildlife out there, stirring. The other lives.

As the milk float ambled along the bottles jiggled in their grid of metal crates—convenient cover, in the otherwise silent pre-dawn, for the noise Nolan was making as he squatted to assemble the L115a4. He was fitting a Smith & Becker 4 Klassic hunting scope, very similar to the Smith & Becker 3 Klassic but with a larger objective lens and an illuminated reticle for optimal twilight performance. He paused as the float pulled in to the Mushanaokoji driveway.

"Your turn," said Logan.

Hogan consulted the list. The Mushanaokojis were down for two semi-skimmed, one full fat and half a dozen eggs.

"They want half a dozen eggs," said Hogan.

Logan poked his head out and whispered to Nolan. "Can you pass me half a dozen eggs?"

"Which ones?"

"Any ones. Half a dozen."

Nolan hesitated. "But there's two types. Free range or battery?"

Logan pulled his head back in. "Free range or battery?"

Hogan looked at the list. "Doesn't say." He dropped the page to his lap. "For *heaven's sake*."

"No harm done," said Logan. "We'll give them the free range. I've never heard of anyone objecting to a free range egg."

"Are you listening to this, Phelan?" Hogan hissed, his head poking out of the cab. "Pay close attention, because this is exactly the kind of fuzzy, cavalier thinking that gets people killed." He turned back to Logan and spoke in a tone so drenched in sarcasm that Phelan felt like asking for a towel.

"And the *price*, Logan? Do you think they might object to the *price*, since they may well have ordered the *cheaper* ones, because they were *cheaper*?"

"I suppose they might. Leave them the free range and we'll charge for the cheaper. No harm done."

"Great," said Hogan. "That's just great." He took the milk and eggs to the Mushanaokoji doorstep and returned. Logan had taken the driver seat and off they went. Phelan began her mental preparations; they were closing in on the crossroads now. She checked the smartphone. Target hadn't moved.

The little truck tinkled. They were the old milk bottles—the fat little round-shouldered ones, foil caps glinting white, blue, and red. In the white-tops a layer of rich cream would gather in the neck of the bottle—a treat for the opener who more often than not was a sparrow in the porch. It occurred to her to wonder why that didn't happen in cartons, that layer of cream.

Or did it?

"There's the crossroads," said Nolan.

She needed the bathroom.

W e're all little people, for a start. How could you not have noticed that? Of course you have. And what with there being seven of us, around this central female lead, we just assumed it was some kind of Snow White reboot. Didn't enjoy working with Abby, if I'm honest. Did she tell you she's worked with the greats? Of course she did.

Interpreted through Freud. That was my take, anyway. I mean, it's all there, isn't it? The Oedipus/ Electra mash up. Where is the mother in all of this, after all? Is her conspicuous absence a reference to the evil queen? The stepmother? If Target is the handsome prince, how do we make sense of the final scene?

And what part of the story would constitute the enchanted sleep? The compound? The 'job' that

Phelan refers to? Or all of it—is she, in fact, dreaming? Is someone else dreaming that *they* are Phelan? I was fascinated, personally. For his part, he played his cards very close to his chest. Wouldn't discuss it. I think that's exactly right for this sort of thing, don't you?

The psychoanalytic tropes. Stroking a coiled rope? I mean, come on. The ham sandwich—would that be displacement or sublimation, do you think? Poison apple? And all that anal retention. The interminable lists. The egg thing. Such attention lavished on spurious detail while a central theme remains fugitive. Terribly clever. The end made me cry, I don't mind telling you. It's as if all the mystery dissolves. The symbolism seems to collapse under its own weight. It falls away elegantly, deliberately—revealing what is after all a very simple, even childlike, expression of grief. But apparently no.

"We overspent on the float and all this military hardware," he said. "Not to mention a shit ton of tritium. There was an offer on dwarves."

N olan was on his feet, watching the crossroads through the Smith & Beckers, the smartphone in his other hand. Phelan crouched.

"He's on the move."

Target had vaulted the wall and made a run for it, right to left in Nolan's sights. He threw the phone to Phelan.

"Keep track of him!"

The Four Forty reached the intersection where Logan brought them to a stop. Apart from the garden wall the crossroads was lined with hedge and wooden fences. The one streetlamp, still lit at this hour, bathed everything in its glow as the sky brightened. The scene seemed contrived, as if studio-lit, the daytime augmented by the lamp's long shadows. Fake somehow, or *super* real. Phelan was still down, grimacing. She wanted to go to the toilet.

Nolan was looking at her closely.

"You OK?"

There was nothing judgmental in his voice, but his eyes betrayed a we-don't-have-time-for-this anxiety. "Is your sphincter trembling? You have to clench harder. Squeeze it back up and the convulsions will subside."

She clenched as hard as she could but it wouldn't go back up. This was borderline; the pain was sharp and pressing. She had brought it to the edge like this before but that had been for fun. Now wasn't the time.

"Get up here, Phelan. It has to be you. You have to take the shot."

She couldn't. Beads of sweat were forming. She groaned. Nolan snapped.

"For goodness sake! You should have gone before we came out!"

She breathed. Steadily. Rhythmically. Cullen's exercises. She thought about her brother. About young Tamas Giametti. About sparrows in the porch. At last the urgency retreated. She felt herself get an intestinal hold. She thought about things that were distant until her rectum was no longer in the grip of spasm. Then she stood.

"Take this," said Nolan, handing her the L115a4 and switching to his Leopolds.

She put her eyes to the scope. Nolan was scanning for target.

"Got him?" she asked.

"At the corner of the house. He's—"

The second she had him she let off a couple of rounds. Target went lower, partially obscured now by the hedge beneath the gable. Nolan lowered the Mark 3's. He was pale.

"It's him, Phelan."

"Of course it is." She grinned at him, elated. "Nearly there! It'll be over soon."

"No." His hand was on the rifle. "It's *him*, Phelan. It's your *dad*."

She put her eye back to the Smith & Becker's and peered through the foliage. It was him alright, squatting and breathing heavily. She recognized his jumper; there were a couple of rips in it where she'd hit him.

This was it. She dropped the L114a4 and drew her Hochler & Kick.

"Come on," she said and jumped off the float, making her way directly towards the house, diagonally across next door's garden.

"Phelan, wait!"

When she reached the house his back was against the wall. He hadn't moved, hadn't made any attempt to. His face was grey—no blood in it, nor any around the holes she'd put in him.

Opposite him, the bank of earth that separated the two bungalows. She'd played in it with her brother—a miniature zone of tunnels and plastic toys commandeered for second purposes.

Soldiers.

She cocked her weapon. "Hello Target."

She could make out the blurred, Brownian borders of supposedly sharp things. See the air shimmer where heat rose from the top of his head. Smell the inside of her own nose. Hear every turn of the rotor blades on the chopper that was coming for them. As her finger began to squeeze there was nothing wrong. Not with him, not with her. Each held the other by the eye. No fear. Nothing left to hold onto. It really was over. Uproarious laughter from the boys, the Apache descending, the stool on its final slide, into the light.

Elizabeth Cooperman

Epigraph for an Unwritten Novel

"How unbearable it would be to die—to leave 'scraps,' 'bits,' . . . nothing really finished" (Katherine Mansfield).

. . . though one of these might work better:

"Writing is hot and it hurts and it doesn't make me happy . . ." (Lucie Brock-Broido).

"There are times when I could be physically sick, the stuff's so low" (Flaubert, while composing *Madame Bovary*).

"He declared that his imagination was hidebound; it was there, but it pulled hard. After he got a notion for a story, months passed before he could get any sort of personal contract with it, or feel any potency to handle it . . ." (Willa Cather on Stephen Crane).

"I have not yet made something that TOTALLY pleases me" (from Vija Celmins' diary).

"Even in my brain, in my head, I can think and act and write wonders—wonders; but the moment I really try to put them down I fail miserably" (Mansfield).

"I start with a blank, and there's nothing more *horrifying* than a blank canvas, cause I don't have a thought or idea . . ." (Lee Krasner).

"Think of something . . . Have an idea. A bright idea" (Beckett).

Spoken in the voice of the Sun: "a cloud intervening . . . / would be stronger than I and I be discredited" (Marianne Moore).

"All these people are making their mark in the world, / While I, pigheaded, awkward, / Different from the rest, / Am only a glorious infant still nursing at the breast" (Lao Tzu).

Jean Rhys: "All of writing is a huge lake. There are great rivers that feed the lake, like Tolstoy and Dostoevsky. And there are trickles, like Jean Rhys."

"Therefore, I am not a necessary being" (Blaise Pascal).

"Slowly, to no outcome" (Lyn Hejinian).

"Yesterday was my Birth Day. So completely has a whole year passed, with scarcely the fruits of a *month.*—O Sorrow and Shame . . . I have done nothing!" (Samuel Taylor Coleridge).

"He had been trying to live and think in a way that he hoped would end by making a poet of him, but it hadn't worked" (Katherine Anne Porter).

"No man but a blockhead ever wrote except for money" (Samuel Johnson).

"I have not written anything today worth a sou" (Katherine Mansfield).

"The more books we read, the clearer it becomes that the true function of a writer is to produce a masterpiece and that no other task is of any consequence. Obvious though it should be, how few writers will admit it, or having drawn the conclusion, will be prepared to lay aside the piece of iridescent mediocrity on which they have embarked!" (first two sentences of Cyril Connolly's *The Unquiet Grave*).

"Almost every man wastes part of his life attempting to display qualities which he doesn't possess" (Johnson).

"I am but a link in the chain of heretics and failures, a woodwind solo in the interminable symphony . . ." (Connolly).

"I am irritated by my own writing. I am like a violinist whose ear is true, but whose fingers refuse to reproduce precisely the sounds he hears" (Flaubert).

"nothing but wretchedness and error come from me . . ." (Pascal).

"I am posing here," wrote Katherine Mansfield in her journal, "as a lady with a weak heart and lungs of Spanish leather."

"Thou art infected" (Shakespeare, *The Tempest*).

"To enter your own mind you need to be armed to the teeth" (Paul Valery).

"August 30th: Morning tears return; spirits at their lowest ebb. Approaching forty, sense of total failure: not a writer but a ham actor whose performance is clotted with egotism; dust and ashes" (again Connolly, my melancholy friend).

"Aristotle writes that you'll suffer over the mysteries but will learn nothing new" (Brenda Hillman).

"So far I haven't succeeded. I might not even be a sculptor at all. I feel I don't understand volumes" (Alberto Giacometti).

"Seems like my life has erectile dysfunction" (Mira Gonzalez).

"Had I followed my pleasure and chosen what I plainly have a decided talent for: police spy, I should have been happier than I afterwards became" (Kierkegaard).

"I hope this preamble will soon come to an end" (Beckett).

REVIEW | TREY STRECKER

The Churchgoer
Patrick Coleman
Harper Perennial, July 2019, $16.99

It's the early 2000s in San Diego, and Mark Haines is a broken man, a man whose present exists in stark contrast with his past life as a beloved evangelical pastor who abandoned his faith and his family. Now, Mark surfs and works night-time security at an industrial park, "protect[ing] things no one wants to steal." When a fellow security guard is murdered during a break in and Cindy Liu, a young hitchhiker Mark has befriended, vanishes, he tries to locate the missing girl and is drawn deep into a shady network of surfer punks, drug smugglers, and con men, including the pastor of Canaan Hills, a shiny corporate megachurch that was "what was left if you took God out" of church.

Mark's reflection on his lapsed faith and his pursuit of Cindy allows *The Churchgoer* to explore the gulf between doubt and certainty, "between not-knowing and knowing," and Patrick Coleman skillfully develops the tarnished humanity of his characters without answering all our questions about them. The novel repeatedly asks us to consider how the stories we tell about ourselves and about others can both define and limit who we are because, as Mark observes, "sometimes a story is stronger than a person. Especially a story someone tells about you."

Sharp and stylish with the Southern California noir vibe of Thomas Pynchon's *Inherent Vice*, readers will be pulled in by the novel's gripping conspiratorial plot, Coleman's deft character development, and Mark's cutting, often humorous, critique of American culture and "where California had gone wrong." Thoroughly modern yet steeped in the noir tradition, *The Churchgoer* is a stunning debut.

Thomas Walton

Five Sketches on We

February Can Be Quite Lovely, Too

Through the window this morning, the scent of sarcococca strong and thin. The first warm day of the year. Dad had a heart attack last night.

"He's all right, though," my sisters say over the phone, as if this were somehow good news. The old bastard will suffer through a few more years.

What a dick sunset can be. The cold, they say, will return tomorrow and wither what's been brazen enough to bloom, clinging even now to frost-bitten branches, lingering until winter is, finally, through.

Bury Me in Violins

I don't think I want to be buried here on this suburban lawn, though it's pleasing and the robins seem to never stop singing. Still, some secret garden would be better, a secret barstool even.

Remember when Tuuli used to call robins violins? And how we let her do it? . . . for years? Until she started school and her classmates drove her to conformity. And then the robins seemed less delightful, though still went on singing. I suppose they still are delightful: at once both delightful and, somehow, residual. How every song now is two songs: one the song and one the song within the song. That's where I want to be buried, in a grave that is both grave and gravely duplicitous.

36 Divided by 6 is 6

The nature of contentment, I think, is somewhat like short division. The search for transcendence the same (who amongst us won't, in the end, transcend?). After a time the problem dissolves into its solution. The one becomes the other, and so there's no need to solve or search at all.

I Always Thought "Urethra" Was A Good Name for A Child

From the urgent abstraction forcing us down and turning us over, the sun acted like it was rising, and in so doing spilled into my apartment, flooding it with pink light and illuminating those tiny specks of floating debris as it fell across the bookshelf and seemed to be—the sun, the light—most enamored with the rubber plant and the bright blue/orange spine of Dorothy Parker's Collected Poems.

American Hybrid

I was thinking about the avant-garde when the garbage truck came screaming to a stop outside my window. The garbage man—Doug's brother Darren—leapt out and ran wildly yelling "give me all your soft falling folds and cruel clouds of circus!" Then he pulled out the peonies Jordan and I planted last spring and threw them in his famished machine.

"Darren you bastard!" I yelled out, "I'll beat you yet you irreadable gob of unfeeling language!"

REVIEW | Moira Walsh

Familiars
Holly Wren Spaulding
Alice Greene & Co., Nov. 2020

Singing our siblings—
acorn, boar, heron, brook—
back from estrangement

Steven D. Schroeder

Live Updates

48 posts in the past 24 hours
Sorted old to new

Rumors could spread by breath or touchscreen

Virus might transmit through fecal matter

Inspection of city sewage predicts infection spikes

Disease causes massive gastrointestinal distress

Government's emergency toilet paper reserve disappears

President declares war against contagiousness

Study finds crowds are fine except for people

Nation's shut-ins should feel fucking lucky, some say

You don't get it unless you get it, epidemic skeptic says

Would many, many cases at once reset the meter?

Infection curve becomes a thrilling theme park roller coaster

Economy won't fall if we don't look down

Foreign virus production brought back onshore

States unsure whether to reopen businesses by force

Students return to learning 33% virtual, 33% in person, 33% in purgatory

Experts recommend not coughing into fifty uncovered mouths a minute

Officials debate suggesting protective shrugs

Is an ounce of prevention worse than death?

Too inconvenient to even ask about, prevention survey says

Tests show 50% or less may or may not have or have had infection

Poll shows 50% wouldn't know this symptom if it bit them

Virus could turn random internal organs into goo or maybe glue

Molten gold is a miracle cure, according to commercials

Disease targets losers, according to anonymous sources

Ignore the bodies, according to executive order

To double the number of beds available, hospitals cut and stack

Disturbing minority healthcare disparities update #834

Potential defects investigated in protective shrugs

Study of molten gold injections hints at harmful side effects

Eccentric pharmaceutical firm starts vaccine scavenger hunt

Virus power rankings versus cancer, car wrecks, context

Expertise distrusted, experts claim, but should you trust them?

Study determines unconfirmed reports survive in air for hours

Disease caused by lies, president alleges without evidence

Opinions differ on drinking molten gold for health

Wealthy megadonors to wallow in vaccine dose pool

Tracking shows cases coming closer and closer

Tracking shows cases coming from inside the house

Virus might be hiding behind you as you read this

How long before your clenched chest is more than worry?

Study discovers your space compresses a little each night

Why the recurring dream where you can only mime goodbye?

Distant has a different definition now

Is what is what will be or will what was be again?

Virus might transmit if you think about it

Virus variant might transmit if you don't think about it

Everything you thought you knew has changed

Too normal could be the newest warning sign

Yahia Lababidi

From Quarantine Notes

Pandemics are also tests of emotional intelligence.

Patriotism, today, is to be ashamed of one's country.

Tell me, how can you tell the difference between bed bugs and the bite of conscience?

There is something boring about evil; it is finite.

Art for art's sake is a dead end; art for heart's sake is the way out.

Inspiration speaks in fits and starts—revealing to us only what is necessary, at the time.

As a profession, constructing sentences is as honorable as building homes—if we and others can live in them.

What is *not* a writing prompt?

To build up your capacity to say No, begin in your dreams.

Aphorisms are the sushi of literature.

Revolution is a kind of drunkenness, like love. It's difficult to revisit our sentiments, sober, when it's over.

Vastness: our only way out of this narrow-hearted mess . . .

Strange, shifting heart . . . breathlessly, panting after the world in the early morning and, sublimely, rid of it by afternoon.

Sometimes, desperation can look like courage.

Walk so that you don't frighten small birds away.

Take your dreams, seriously, they represent unfinished work. But, don't take them too seriously—they represent unfinished work.

Sometimes, the crack in everything lets the light in—other times, its darkness.

Without silliness, no seriousness.

Words seem to reinvent us just as we think we are inventing them.

We are haunted by the ghosts of who we meant to be.

Daniel Beauregard

After Kafka

I'd like to return this mirror if I may, says a man, struggling with a large mirror in his hands.

And what seems to be the problem with this particular mirror? the clerk in the complaints department asks without looking up.

I can't see myself in it, that's the problem. The more I look at it, the more I realize I could never see myself in such a mirror. No . . . no, not this one, it's just not possible, and it certainly wasn't cheap.

The salesperson seems taken aback, then vaguely gestures he'll return in a moment, shuffling off into a darker corner of the office.

A strong, towering man with a fiery red beard emerges from the shadows and takes the place where the previous clerk was sitting, the chair groaning beneath his weight.

Now what seems to be the problem?

As I explained to your associate, this mirror doesn't work.

What, doesn't work, you say?

The man scratches his beard in thought then stands up from behind the desk, crossing to the front of the room where the other man stands nervously, still struggling to hold the heavy mirror.

Prop it up there—the other man says, pointing to a nearby chair—let's have a look.

The nervous man props the mirror up against the chair.

Both stand back and look.

After a moment, the man with the fiery beard exclaims:

By Christ you're right; my head's been cut clean off!

The heavy mirror then suddenly slid off the chair onto the floor, shattering into a multitude of pieces. Horrified, the nervous man got down on his hands and knees, hurriedly picking up the shards until he froze—each one bore his face in varying degrees, but none the precise one he was looking for.

Alina Stefanescu

Reading Kafka in the Parabolic Time of Pandemic

Pandemic time, like pandemic space, is both endless and claustrophobic: we live in narrow rooms with the remembered simulacra of others, the vestige of scents and tactile sensations, the terror of crowds alongside the loneliness. Franz Kafka's parables have been good company in this dread-inflected space. The immaculate thought-rooms of *Parables and Paradoxes* draw the eye away from the astonished of streets and empty sidewalks, the costumes of masks, the binaries of threat and kindness, the eugenicist undertone of many pandemic policies legislated by states to ensure the safety of the "fittest."

❧

On the day when my oldest child wept realizing there would be no kisses and physical touching in his 11th grade year of virtual schooling, I read "On Parables," which thinks through the assumption that parables are useless in "daily life, which is the only life we have." Kafka ends with a conversation between two men which focuses around what winning resembles, and whether the moral aim of the parable extends to us in life. The second man says he loses in the world what he wins in the parable. The first replies, "No, in reality: in parable you have lost." Extending the parable to ordinary life is only a win in the world of the daily. The story we use to make moral sense of events feels immoral on the ground.

❧

On the day twitter blazes with longing for pedicures, I read "Pekin and the Emperor," and discover a point of convergence in the end: "To set about establishing a fundamental defect here would mean undermining not only our consciences, but, what is far worse, our feet."

❧

On the day a man uses his powerful leafblower to move leaves from the neighbor's yard to our own, on the day this man backs his truck into the fence beside our front window and tears part of it down, I meet the "The Imperial Colonel" who rules a small mountain town. The imperial gaze is the power which causes subjects to obey a despot. Humans offer their obedience to an evil leader because his gaze, like that of a god, does not include them—it renders them puppets or playthings, parts of set. This gaze "a nonchalant, roving, and yet steady gaze, a gaze with which one might, for instance, observe the movements of a crowd in the distance," and the presence of the "indefinable smile" on the Imperial Colonel's face alternates between "irony" and "dreamy reminiscence." Outside of time, the gaze sees everything, reduces persons to an eschatological end, the fulfillment of something a subject can only suspect.

❧

On the day an extended family member posts a meme about how Biden will tear down the walls that protect us from Mexican immigrants, I wander into "The Great Wall and the Tower of Babel," which begins with the "news of the building of the tall wall" penetrating the now of the world. The parable's narrator returns to his ten-year old self, recalling a day with his father in "the smallest circumstances." The big event, here, is broken down into the impressions of a young rememberer; the tremendous meets the tiny in time. What matters is that the father held his hand, and this relationship of proximity to the father blurs the line between the world as experienced by the son and the world as declaimed by a parent. The narrator describes the emperor's pigtail, eating soup, staring at things, and then ends this small piece with what his father had reported "from the threshold of that moment," which he offers in a "verbatim" memory that colludes with other things circulating in that time, and space, suggesting that a child's memory must be fragment, must pull things together into parabolic objects with the words of the father at the end:

> Thus, my father said more or less the following: a strange boatman—I know all those who usually sail past here, but this one was a stranger—has just told me that a great wall is going to be built to protect the Emperor. As you may know, the infidel nations, with demons among them too, often gather in front of the Imperial Palace and shoot their black arrows at the emperor.

The problem with building that Tower of Babel to heaven lies in the city, or the builders. Kafka explores this in "The City Coat of Arms," which pivots around the symbolism in a coat of arms that includes, strangely, a fist. As the people attempt to build the Tower, they realize it will not be finished in their lifetimes. Suddenly, the task lacks immediacy, the buy-in dissolves over questions of housing and status: "Every nationality wanted the finest quarters for itself." Faced with the infinite or eternity, humans seek more pressing troubles, like social comparison, envy, the feel of the stadium. The little fights developed into wars, and then new fights, with constant outbursts and calls for vengeance, and with each increased technical skill or invention, "the occasion for conflict" multi-plied. The parable ends with the fist's unpacking: "All the legends and songs that came to birth in that city are filled with longing for a prophesied day when the city would be destroyed by five successive blows from a gigantic fist. It is for that reason too that the city has a closed fist on its coat of arms." The city's end is inscribed in its story of origin, preserved in the relic of the fist on the coat of arms.

❧

ON THE DAY when I realize vaccinated friends are purchasing their spring break airline tickets and celebrating their election by fine dining experiences, the voluptuous "Green Dragon" enters the room of my envy, saying: "Drawn hither by your longing, I come pushing myself along from afar off, and underneath am now scraped quite sore." He is happy to do it, the green dragon assures me, happy to help me locate myself in comparison to others in the virtue of envy by the gleam of the lottery bin known as modern life.

❧

IN THE WEEK I cannot stop crying and hiding from my children the reality of delayed treatments, I find myself in "Paradise," smack in the scathing succulence of Eden's paradox, where "we are sinful not merely because we have eaten of the Tree of Knowledge, but also because we have not yet eaten of the Tree of Life." For Kafka, we are sinful without being guilty; we are wrong without being designated "criminals." Our expulsion from Paradise did not destroy Paradise—and by our sin, we saved Paradise.

"Why do we lament over the fall of Man? We were not driven out of paradise because of it, but because of the tree of life, that we might not eat of it." The expulsion from Paradise is "the eternal recapitulation of the occurrence," which places us there, "in actual fact," regardless of whether we realize it in the present. This Kafka-time infuses the strange hoops of pandemic, where we juggle the guilt of possibly infecting others with an invisible, silent virus that may be asymptomatic. Aren't we all asymptomatic when it comes to original sin?

The serpent promised "equality with God" to those who ate from the tree; and the serpent kept half that promise, as "man did not become like God", man became like "divine knowledge." A man could think like God—could invent citizenship, build walls to protect purity, and also feel his conscience—despite coding errors "in the original fettering." Because we are equal in our knowledge of Good and Evil—because the fall granted us this equality as a condition—we humans have elected morality as the space in which to display "our individual superiority." What the serpent gave us is half the story of God, or the story of the serpent's frustration: to know good but be unable to fulfill it.

IN THE LOCKED BATHROOM of the week of vast weeping, the virtue signal is already here, in Paradise, in Kafka's fragments and prisons, since the knowledge requires action, or action in accordance with it, even if man has not been given the strength to do so, lacking that part of God—"he must destroy himself trying." So man pulls back in fear of his own weakness, even though "the accomplished cannot be annulled, but only confused. It was for this purpose that our rationalizations were created," Kafka surmises. We create costumes and identities to collude in our self-delusion which we then translate or hand down to bind others. And oh, the virtuosity of the virtue in being able to tell another person that they are failing to be ideal. We celebrate our expertise in diagnosing that very failure.

The theorist is the winner, since the action is made irrelevant by our weakness. As for the visible world, it is "nothing more than a rationalization of a man who wants to find peace for a moment," Kafka continues, "an attempt to falsify the actuality of knowledge, to regard knowledge as a goal still to be reached." It is the exceptions of theory which are the truest, the most relevant to mankind, or homo sapiens sapiens: the species of mammal that writes books to excuse his selfishness while narrowing the banks of his own insignificance. If we cannot be good, we can at least assume the status of minor gods in diagnosing the badness of others.

ON THE DAY of the bear in Transylvania, which is groundhog day in Alabama, I discover other shadows attached to mammals in fragments from Simone Weil's 1943 notebooks, where she considers self-replicating cycles of oppression. "Thus Marx, exactly in the same way as the businessmen of his time or the warriors of the Middle Ages, arrived at a morality which places the social category to which he belonged—that of professional revolutionaries—above sin." Weil marvels at how Marx stumbled into replicating the structures he despised. Relations of dominance create oppressive structures no matter who helms the apparatus of revolt. Dialectical materialism moved from the assumption that, because force rules human relations, injustice is perpetuated by systems, and yet, Marx also insisted that "the weak, while remaining the weak, will nevertheless be the stronger." This eschatological heaven of avenging angels is hard to locate on the ground, or hard to separate from defining justice as the power to punish others. The heart of all prisons lies in this.

As Weil notes, "Marx believed in miracles without believing in the supernatural." From the theoretical framework rooted in rationalism, Weil sees a discontiguousness. She concludes that "if one believes in miracles, it is better to believe in God as well." Both the bear and the groundhog fail to see their shadows this year.

❧

ON THE DAY the church put our Black, unmarried, openly gay rector on administrative leave for caressing another man outside of holy matrimony, I find something unbidden in "The Coming of the Messiah," where Kafka tells us when time will end, when the eschatologies will be fulfilled: "The Messiah will come as soon as the most unbridled individualism of faith becomes possible—when there is no one to destroy this possibility and no one to suffer its destruction; hence the graves will open themselves." At question is the nature of messianic salvation itself, which claims to both end the world and redeem it for another one no one can see, describe, or claim. For "the Messiah will come only when he is no longer necessary; he will come only on the last day after his arrival; he will come, not on the last day, but on the very last." The last-est. The last beyond the possibility of lasting.

❧

ON THE DAY my youngest daughter decides to set her invisible horse free in a meadow outside Birmingham, I find "Abraham," a man born into all the privileges that made him a prophet. Kafka suggests this privilege of house, wife, land, and status may be the reason Abraham needs something taken from him. But it is the other Abrahams, the unrealized Abes, who interest the author: the ones with half-built homes, the son-less ones with nothing to offer Mount Moriah, the clever ones

who read "magic trilogies" so that their houses would not "be in order" and to block the view of the mountain in the distance. Among these alternative Abrahams, there is also the one who fears starting out as Abraham and winding up as Don Quixote—since who knows where the journey might take you? Kafka posits Abraham the fool — "the unsummoned one"—who goes even though not called: "And perhaps he had made no mistake at all, his name really was called, it having been the teacher's intention to make the rewarding of the best student at the same time a punishment for the worst one."

❧

ON THE DAY we move snails from the front steps back to the nearby soil, I encounter a 2011 lecture where Judith Butler touches on the parables in the context of Kafka's estate. "Who Owns Kafka?" visits the ongoing conflict over Kafka's letters and papers between his family estate and the National Library of Israel. At issue is Kafka's legacy—what he wished to mean inseparable from what we take him to say. The German state prefers to claim him as purely German. Czech scholars lodge their own complaints about leaving out Prague. Butler situates this conflict in the Kafkaesque context of rising bureaucracies which track, classify, and measure individuals according to demographic, ethnic, religious, and linguistic criteria. Yiddish, German, and Czech converge in Kafka—he, himself, exists as an outskirt of that quest for purity which bureaucracy has made possible, down to the blood.

The fight over legacy is not a fight over Kafka's legacy so much as which nation gets to use it as an accessory for cultural needs. If Kafka's words have a legacy, perhaps it is precisely the way multilingualism, religion, and the claims of multinationalism unsettle one another in the modern state's administrations of justice, a relationship which has been problematic from the start. For Butler, there is irony in how Kafka's words have been monetized, purified, and reconstructed to suit the needs of nation-states and their capitalist octopus arms.

What Butler calls "the poetics of non-arrival," the gaping, infinite distance between departure and arrival in human time, is present in Kafka's parables. She borrows Benjamin and Adorno's use of the word "gestures" to evoke "stilled moments" and statements which move without enacting, thus severing the tie between speaking and doing, and holding us in their unfinishedness. The gesture reveals the gap in the gaze. The Messiah's time of arrival does not exist in human time, but in the absolution of its ending.

ON THE DAY my last living parent receives a vaccine, I meet "The Emperor," himself, the embodiment of absolute power leveraging sacralization. The emperor may be "our rightful sovereign" and bearer of "divine mission," but what if he's not the descendant of gods? What if he isn't born into divinity but rather the construction of it? Kafka's narrator carries this doubt which does not change the world, doesn't stir anything, as "when the surf flings a drop of water onto the land, that does not interfere with the eternal rolling of the sea, on the contrary, it is caused by it." I can't read the hours from the eras, the pandemic from the prophecy, the end from the beginning of what is to come.

Kevin Boniface

Our Faithful Friend, Micky

Out on delivery the snow covered driveways are marked with the tracks of cats, dogs, Audis and milkmen.

I can smell the aspirational young couples on their lockdown walks from fifty yards away. They Marc Jacobs their way along the lanes arm in arm, kicking leaves in their regulation black quilted jackets, skinny jeans and yoga pants.

The mail box that Mr Smith made and painted gold in honour of the London Olympics in 2012 has weathered over the years. These days it is what it is, a rusty old biscuit tin with a bent lid screwed to a broken fence.

Some cows have escaped into Hawcliffe Lane. The farmer, who is ankle deep in mud is trying to fasten the gate and secure the rest of the herd. I wind down my window and he shouts to me as I pass. "Just ease past 'em. Just ease past 'em. If they go, you go and I'll round em up on t'quad. It's t'only way to do it".

At the next farm on the valley side I go looking for the farmer. I can hear music coming from the stables so I walk up through the mud with an attentive German Shepherd for company. I wander in through the doors and find six horses listening to Phillip Schofield advising them to contact We Buy Any Car Dot Com. There's no sign of the farmer or her assistant and both the exercise bikes in the corner by the sink are unoccupied. I ask the German Shepherd whether he knows where they are but he doesn't reply.

At the Manor House I leave the mail on the step and weigh it down with the rock provided.

At Badger Croft a plastic robin is perched on the fat ball suspended from the bird table.

Mr Briggs pulls over next to me in his Nissan Juke. He winds down the passenger side window, leans across and shouts "T'jobs fucked, i'n't it?" "How come?" I say. "You can't have anyone round, you can't do owt." "Oh, yeah," I say. "See ya, lad," says Mr Briggs and he winds up his window and speeds away.

The woman at the bungalow has some visitors in masks. They are waving to her from her driveway. "I haven't left the house since last March!" she shouts through the kitchen window.

The sanitisation station at the dairy is housed on an old melamine desk, limping on loose legs in the cow shit. It comprises a large dented aluminium bowl and a litre bottle of sanitiser. In the garden over the road, next to the model of a stricken galleon foundering in an old Belfast sink, two care workers in plastic pinnies and visors exchange handover pleasantries and bin liners. Next door, a blonde haired woman in sweatbands and pink lycra is in the middle of a noisy online workout session.

In the village, shards of frost shattered terracotta crunch under my feet and by mid-morning the lanes are busying with dog walkers. Puffa jackets, yoga pants, terriers and Labradors emerge like a lockdown army from the low sun, vape smoke and mist. Mounted divisions on horseback and e-bike stream by in determined silence and lycra. The ice is finally beginning to thaw under threadbare blankets of warm manure.

Past the house with the life-sized statue of a silver elephant in the garden, past the wall built from rocks painted in the colours of the Indian flag, past the house with the metre-long model of an old iron-clad gunboat in the window—sometimes the gunboat's owner straps it to a specially designed trailer which he attaches to his mobility scooter. He then parades the boat around laps of the estate. I once asked the man's wife why he did this and she said "He just likes it to go out every now and again".

Most people on this estate have retired and I spend much of the morning prising open frozen letterboxes to deliver puzzler books and catalogues advertising plastic statuettes for the garden, many of which light up. The pervading odour is that of liver and onions with notes of washing powder. Standing next to a meerkat sitting on a fake rock with a lamp embedded into it, three women in anoraks are discussing anoraks.

Through the icy graveyard, past the big shiny helium love heart stuck in a tree. Past the mouldy VW Camper that hasn't moved for years.

Water vapour plumes from the boiler flues of the new estate where moulded finials finish plastic sash-look Juliette windows at the house of the jet wash entrepreneur.

"Just another day in lockdown!" says the woman who is hosing down a sheep on her front step as I open her gate.

In Andrew Crescent the starlings are Swanee whistling in the trees. A man strides past with collar-length grey hair, long fringe swept to the left in a side parting over large black plastic rimmed glasses. He wears a big beige anorak, grey flannels and hush puppies. Maybe he's on his way to the Crucible theatre to watch the snooker in 1979 or perhaps he's going to interview Ingemar Stenmark on a Sony Trinitron with a collection of Wade Whimsies on the top. The starlings fly off over the garden gravestone of Our Faithful Friend Micky who died in 2002.

Dawn Raffel

Five Stories

The City of Holes

The holes are of varying widths and of un-tapped depths, a matrix of shimmering vacancies, great vaults of absence.

Every living being in the city of holes is held together and connected by holes. Captain of industry. Captain of air. Sailor, baker, mother, lover. Dog, wolf, root, twig. Particle and element.

Bird. Nest.

A hole is not grief. A hole has no language. Yearning, you think, or possibility, but these are only words, with no home in a hole.

The holes in the city of holes cannot be filled by any nameable substance: solid, viscous, fluid, verbal, angel, gas. A hole is not a color.

The city of holes is not a city, of course, which is why it has no limits.

The All-New Sanitary City

Sneezing is illegal in the Sanitary City. Also unlawful are sniffling, drooling, sweating, and sighing. Kissing! Verboten. All of the walls in the sanitary city are stainless, wiped on the hour. Sheets on the beds are made of paper, all the mattresses are glass. Many people come to the sanitary city for refuge from bodily fluid. Menstruation has been ended. Every insemination is mechanical. There is no fear in the sanitary city, no sorrow, no want, no unintended consequence. Nothing may swim from one life to another. Nothing may float from the breath to the ear.

Hades

Persephone could tell you, that fistful of pomegranate seeds wasn't worth it. Ecstasy is fleeting. Night after night, she is biding her time in this darkness where even the dead have ambitions. And why would they not? Pride outlasts the body. Even self-loathing is a form of hubris.

Where Graves Have No Names

In a city in Europe, a cemetery holds only stones, with no coffins, no bodies beneath them. The stones were re-homed in order to make the original graveyard a field for athletics. For reasons of efficiency, perhaps, or decorum, or sanitary practices, officials of the city in question decided to leave bodies interred. Now children kick balls over bones of the dead.

There is no map, no key to the cemetery holding no coffins. Some stones are polished, carved with the letters of a language no longer in use. Some stones are wordless markers of grief. And what of the pebbles, the feathers, the bent blades of grass?

The Writer

She covered her face. She tore the damp stuffing out of the past and filled her fists with synonyms. Flung words like confetti, like fairytale feathers, repeating herself again and again.

She believed, in this way, she could bring back the dead, if just this once.

'A Hole in Every Boy'

After the Sun
Jonas Eika, tr. Sherilyn Nicolette Hellberg
Lolli Editions, August 2021, £12.99

Jonas Eika is the youngest ever winner of the Nordic Council Literature Prize and its most outspoken. His eloquent attack on the Danish prime minister, Mette Frederiksen, who was in the audience at the award ceremony, went viral. Since his novel *Marie House Warehouse* debuted in 2015, Eika has won every major prize in Denmark. *After the Sun*, a collection of four extended short stories, has been translated with sensitive musicality for the UK and US—who arguably stand to benefit more from his message: that inequality diminishes us all.

These are stories of yearning that keen from a globalised world where even the successful are exploited by the dehumanising forces of the market. The settings are scattered and familiar, but they take us to unpredictable, fantastical places, vehicles for the ineffable pain of modern life on the margins. In 'Bad Mexican Dog', Cancun beach boys suffer the injustices of violent, narcissistic tourists, by night enacting arcane erotic rituals. 'Rachel, Nevada' dwells in the 'peculiar and elastic time' near Area 51, where a grief-stricken Antonio tries to fuse himself with an alien machine—a thing that can scream the exact vibration howl of his misery. In 'Me, Rory and Aurora' a troubled London threesome falls into drugs and danger under the quasi-religious influence of social services contracted to a private company. 'Alvin' is the tale of an ex-pat Dane who, finding that the Copenhagen bank where he is to work has collapsed, goes on to have a strange encounter with a derivatives trader.

Ground down by the transactional thrust of late capitalism, Eika's characters rise through unearthly ritual: the dance of the unconscious, as those oppressed seek the uncanny, seek to transcend their surroundings and access their desires in a post-god world. By no means the least weird of these rituals is that of two men scanning futures derivatives on a laptop in bed, the act of which successfully removes the protagonist of 'Alvin' from his new bodily location: 'I felt at home, and had completely forgotten that we were in Romania.'

Alienation is central, and expressed in language that has a psychic, prophetic beauty. Characters are removed from themselves, crazed by feelings they don't understand, that can't be heard in the world as it is. A Cancun tourist, exploited in turn by those she exploits laments, 'every time you're reminded of what happened, it feels like somebody else's bad feelings, but you're the one who has to feel them, you can never leave your body all the way.' Yet this distance from one's own flesh is what Antonio of 'Rachel, Nevada' must achieve in order to perform the gruesome operation involved in becoming the machine. Sadness descends physically: 'a big, greywhite feeling, and at its edge hovered a dark object that I couldn't grasp,' in 'Alvin'; in 'Bad Mexican Dog' as a beach boy walks away from an abusive tourist he finds that 'the cold has crept into my back, which she can't see, and turned into a hole inside me.' Later, he understands that 'there's a hole in every boy'—like the Dane's sensation of 'dark matter contracting into itself', like the 'dark and clear metallic dissonance' of the screaming desert machine, like the 'hunger and numbness' after the high in 'Rory, Aurora and me.'

If that is the black void in us all, Eika's fiction suggests where the light may creep in, in our unintended tender moments where we reach each other, despite it all. In 'Alvin', the protagonist is assailed by feelings of joy lying next to the trader. In 'Rory, Aurora and Me' the threesome simulates family life: a homeless young girl is Rory and Aurora's surrogate child (with whom they have sex); Rory cleans, tidies and makes soup (with stolen vegetables) while 'Mum' goes to work (selling drugs by the church gate to rehab inmates). In 'Bad Mexican Dog', a beach boy, Manu, seems to have 'crustaceans and mottled fish swimming around in the shell of his pelvis, in the light blue ocean lapping against his pubic bone.' In the boys' rituals, such mystical sea power becomes capable of restoring even life: 'I can't separate my own voice from the others' assholes from the hole deeper inside me where the pain and foreign blood run down hollow parasol shafts soaking the sandy soil below the basin.' A kind of magic rises, an orange light that traces through the stories, the feeling that all this must lead to a new dawn, a new way of living.

Each perfectly crafted story takes us down the rabbit hole from hyperrealism to surrealism. Which better expresses our reality? Our relationship with the incorporeal is increasingly complicated, as symbolised by the bank in 'Alvin'—somehow still functioning, even as rubble. The derivatives trading feels as 'fictional' to the protagonist as the flight to Copenhagen, yet the effect of both is physically real. In 'Rachel, Nevada', Eika draws direct attention to this paradox as Antonio considers the 'demeaning form of consolation' of calling his dead daughters' voicemails: 'at once so unreal in the breathless telephone receiver and corporeal with the sounds of their moving tongues and mouths, amplified by the microphone's compressor.' This is our reality today as we live online, merge with machines and bank on ether. There are invisible forces controlling our behaviour, leaving us removed from our own souls.

In *The Spirit Level: Why Equality is Better for Everyone* Richard Wilkinson and Kate Pickett ask: 'How is it that we have created so much mental and emotional suffering despite levels of wealth and comfort unprecedented in human history?' In *After the*

Sun Eika explores this question with urgency, seeing deep into the damage to the human psyche, flinging its most secret, desperate longings to the stars and becoming his own alien mouthpiece for humanity's continuous scream.

JESI BENDER

PORTRAIT OF Emmett TILL

Mama wanted to show them
how a face can become mud
bubblin'

Hung me on a drying rack
to air the horror human
hands make

My face is gravel my face
is blind my face is movement human so
unkind

O yes I can still whisper my secrets
without a tongue

O yes I can still whistle like a spate
with all this water in my lungs

The Dregs of the Day
Máirtín Ó Cadhain, tr. Alan Titley
Yale University Press (Margellos World Republic of Letters),
Sept. 2019, $13.00

Brief Lives of Idiots
Ermanno Cavazzoni, tr. Jamie Richards
Wakefield Press, December 2020, $14.95

In 2015, Ó Cadhain's most celebrated novel *Cré na Cille* appeared for the first time in two English translations (*The Dirty Dust* and *Graveyard Clay*), triggering an ecstasy of squeeing among fans of neglected modernist masterpieces and Irish literature devotees clamouring for something other than new monographs on Beckett or Flann O'Brien. That novel, a multitude of voices from beyond the grave helmed by the hysterical Caitriona Puadeen, took place entirely among the dead: a frenetic stream of insults, hearsay, banter, prattle, and bickering, flitting from one enraged corpse to the next. Now, translator Alan Titley returns with Ó Cadhain's final work, a despairing novella taking place over the course of one day, a flagrant anti-*Ulysses* where a man named N. staggers around an unnamed town unable to make the arrangements in the wake of his wife's death.

The novella unravels like a less spirited version of J.P. Donleavy's *The Ginger Man*—a teeter-tottering anti-picaresque of wobbling from one whiskey to the next as N. seeks to flee the coppers in pursuit for neglecting his wife's carcass. Finding refuge in the arms of the rotund Squimzy, N. reflects on the vagaries and vulgarities of 1960s Ireland. In prose that mixes the vernacular, caustic commentary, and internal monologue, the novella depicts an Ireland in a state of stasis, a nation exhausted by years of religious observation and social propriety (esp. the choking hold of the civil service), a place moored in greyness and soaked in whiskey. For N., as for so many Irish, the prospect of emigrating to America, a land where dollars parodically drip from the trees, is the only release from the nightmare of his homeland.

The Dregs of the Day is a work from a mind at the end of its tether—cynical, choleric, mordantly chucklesome, a festival of droch-aimsir.

Our access to idiocy in the Year of Our Lord 2021 is unlimited. The frothing violence of idiots, waging a war on 300,000 years of sweet evolutionary progress is a mere subtweet away—an endlessly self-replenishing scroll of unpunctuated doltitude commonly only seen in the yowling of former American presidents. Ermanno Cavazzoni's collection, first published in 1994, is a condensed cackle of cretinism, containing a full calendar month's worth of stories drawn from historical accounts—a veritable Wunderkammer of dumpkofferies. As a member of the Italian Oulipo spin-off OpLePo—a workshop of potential literature drawing on linguistic and structural constraints for maximum imaginative voltage—Cavazzoni has constructed an exquisite pastiche of Alban Butler's *The Lives of the Saints*.

Among the idiots are included a family who throw stones in the air to better comprehend the phenom of gravity (many of which clobber their skulls on comedown), a mathematical prodigy whose brilliance falters when writing verse, a tenant farmer who practices medicine as a hobby until a blood pressure gauge is fixed too tightly around his mother's neck, and a realist writer who tries to incorporate every banal movement into his novel. The tales also chronicle unfortunates rather than idiots, such as the lists of suicides with collateral damage, the obese woman with paranoid diarrhoea, and the man whose fondness for a fake nose sparks political upheaval. Pathos, hilarity, tragedy and blackly comic slapstick abound in this glorious gallery of numpties, translated and introduced exquisitely by Jamie Richards.

The Notebooks of John Robert Colombo
The Battered Silicon Dispatch Box, 5 vols.,
2311 pages, $150.00

I should confess at the beginning that the Canadian poet John Robert Colombo (b. 1936) has been for some four decades now my closest literary colleague. Though we've actually met less than ten times, always in his native Toronto, we've been in constant touch, initially by postal mail, more recently by email. The best reason for my reviewing his monumental *Notebooks* (2018, five volumes) is that I doubt if anyone else in another country (aka the USA) will.

Prodigiously productive with books, always from publishers based in his native country, Colombo has published over the past six decades collections of his poetry and translations in addition to anthologies of Canadian poetry and the supernatural and then several Canuck "reference" mausolea, including *Colombo's Canadian Quotations* (1994), *Colombo's Canadian References* (1976), *Colombo's Book of Canada* (1978), and *The Dictionary of Canadian Quotations* (1991), which all have the distinction of being books that nobody else, not even another Canadian, could have compiled, even if they tried. Produced before he obtained a personal computer, these were produced, heroically we can now say, on cards 3" by 5". (A favorite anecdote recalls how a publisher contracting one of these books tried to put *its own name* in place of Colombo's in the title. After Colombo took home his manuscript that was subsequently released by another house, the offending publisher later commissioned a competitor with its name in the title. Inferior, it stunk and sank.) Oh yes, this Canuck writes in English, clean English, albeit with occasional Anglican spellings.

Having encountered around the year 2000 a "publishing block," as he correctly calls it,

Colombo has been mostly self-sponsoring ever since. His masterpiece is *Self-Schrift* (first edition 1999), which is a frequently updated compendium (2007, 2015) of "commentaries—anecdotes, insights, appreciations, criticism, ideas, and theories" about the dozens of books published under his name. Every writer should produce this sort of book, even if only fractionally as prolific. Another exemplary move has been modest self-issued annuals of Colombo's miscellaneous writings from the previous year.

From a supportive small book publisher, curiously named Battered Silicon Dispatch Box, with addresses in both Ontario and Wisconsin, now comes *The Notebooks of John Robert Colombo* in five volumes with over one million words, totaling over 2300 pages in sum. These books contain a rich amount of commentary and information on a great variety of subjects, most of it engagingly written as well as easily skimmed; so that once I began the first volume, I stayed up well past my bedtime to finish it. Later I've read all five at a beach between fits of swimming.

One theme is the immense range of Colombo's experience, or at least of what he chooses to write about; and this in turn reflects his extraordinary powers of understanding. As a writer he seems to be, in Henry James's words, "One of those people on whom nothing is lost." As these five printed books lack an index, be relieved that the generous publisher promises to "provide the purchaser with a searchable PDF" on request.

His favorite subjects are Canada and Canadians (and particularly Toronto and Torontonians) about which his curiosity and knowledge are bottomless. His *Notebooks* include not only thumbnails of both his literary colleagues and historic politicians, but much (new to me) about supernatural experiences, which became the stuff of a few dozen Colombo anthologies. Surprised I was to learn of his lifelong interest in the forever unfashionable century-old ideas of G. I. Gurdjieff and P. D. Ouspensky.

Because Colombo was initially a poet, rather than, say, a newspaperman, whatever he has to say comes at a length most appropriate for his thought. So some entries are a short paragraph, while others run for several pages. Because he was never an academic or otherwise an institutional factotum, he's an exemplary free-spirit. In one of his more audacious moves Colombo counts the number of times his and his wife Ruth of sixty years have made love. (As it's nearly 15,000, shouldn't this be noticed in *World Records* or, at least, biographical encyclopedias of writers?)

Since he long ago copyedited other authors' books for Toronto publishers, I was surprised to find "principle" repeatedly confused with "principal" and then whole entries duplicated and, in one case, even triplicated, sometimes just a few pages apart. (Too bad he didn't show this to me *before* printing? Tsk, tsk.) Since Colombo gathered his entries by subject, rather than chronology, say, I wish he'd put the dates of original authorship at the beginning, rather than at the end, which was sometimes too many pages away.

May others enjoy knowing Colombo, if not as personally as I have, because his writings will survive him, as will this book. He's a Canadian treasure that can be successfully exported, if less lucratively than furs and oil. Indeed, literary immortality should be the aim of any writer productive past the age of 80, as Colombo is. Likewise, the measure of any ambitious small publisher should be sponsoring books likely to survive their authors, as the best books can do, especially at a time when pre-owned books have become so plentifully available over the Internet.

Colin James

Two Poems

PERRY MORPHOUS SINGS THE HITS

His home studio was a bit echoey,
gave him his famous vibrato
getting out of the way of sound.
Eventually he sought refuge
in the quiet island fields
and seasonally silent vineyards.
He had a backup group for a time,
The Maidens, but their sandals
made him unable to concentrate.
His muse was an acrobat
half man and half goat
who worked mostly in the cliffs.
He played the lyre like a god
while retaining an earthly reverb.
This selection of famous songs
is only available during this offer.
So go to your phones and call us.
We may not respond right away
that's the way it goes with myths.

THOUGHT HE WAS SPENCER TRACY

He watched the old movie channels
from a tall blade of grass together
with his closest friends.
The wind was unkind and then not.
He learned how to read lips in preschool
one syllable at a time,
effusively thanked the old butterfly a lot.
Preferred white cotton suits
to the dreary authoritative smock.
Told his peers to approach it circuitously
become smaller and smaller quietly
until disappearing into the light.

Duodenal Etiquette, Scènes de Ballet

Punch, with paddle
Judy, without paddle

Punch:

Perfection? Pfui! Return it to peerless source!
She cooks, gavottes, blue spark as clean as, in liquidity awash,
but nay I say, she will not do.
Bring on the lady's twin, Aurora Sunset Midday Yin
(no kin to yen, currency or urge), followed by Ying,
& better than either or even forever, & so on, etcetera,
at last enmeshed where Quotidia tugs
tasseled gliss&i & frolicsome bugs. (Whack!)

I dashed off in haste: Mere moments away from ominous pings,
accountancy's fugues, essence of otter,
Destiny's tutus encircling daughters,
palpability's badinage,
a fusillade by spasms arrayed,
alighting lightly on the splayed,
a setting for a gropes, by which crass device the race lopes along
as deconstructs the deck callèd poop. I hear you, Hosanna,
a Mae West requesting out there in the saline goop,
your spinto urgencies surplusly befouling
aqueous frills in the deep's embrace.
One squints to intuit tomorrow's erasures,
comes away with an ardent Inuit,
excellent benefits, perks. (Whack!)

Judy:

Ere we befouled our bespoke jodhpurs
merest motes in th'aether were, disfiguring matter
with imprecise skills.

Read into gestures ends before spleens,
dirigible dreams,
dank motets in bile braised,
sutured harmonics, anchors aweighed.

Can bunting mask an assassin's world-view?
Camouflage farts?
Provide the glue for klunky mesostics?
Flat-out erotics?
A Phillips-head screw? (O surly yew!)
Be Hugo Boss's Siegfried line?
A varietal whine? A rheum with ague?

I dashed off in haste: He wears a giant sheetrocker's scowl!
I dashed off in haste: He brandishes a two-ton trowel!
I dashed off in haste: At anti-matter he fusses & fumbles,
stately as portals to outst&ing venues,
bigger even than tectonic bungles!
Stuffing feathers up his nose!
Inhaling! Inhaling! Feathers no more!

Punch:

J'adore your leg. (Whack!)
I note the point at which your leg tolerates anything,
an observation I file under Marvels Relating to Limbs.
Other possibilities?
Ramen Lao Da's Ramen Da Xiao,
Jie's Ramen One Thing / Two,
Crayfish Ramen,
Raimondo's stew bleu.

After the rain, gazing at the glistening treetops,
his sister mutters dreamily, "Aspen, aspirin,
aspersions cast & casting . . ."
He, likewise dreamily, lays his neck athwart a stump
awaiting a hooded passerby,
th'aspens whisp'ring, "Breeze . . ."

I clap clamshells in hope of becoming a percussionist.
I require tutelage.

Two potatoes, three. The aspins' sighs,
this must wait or seem to, pig, & thinking so, see . . . (Whack!)

Judy:

Women almost hear them, swains in pits hastily dug.
Marmots mayhap?
At length we encounter a sky-like expanse
a touch too lacy, too long pants,
a too big hat under which one recalls
st&ing atop a discomfited child, its urgent "Uhn!"
suggesting what? Disaffection?
When I am old enough to ask, you will be dead.

Brighter stars were burning then, in 1692.
Among slate rooftops she abode, up spires shimmying,
herself, I mean, in olden times,
calling softly to yet softer clouds,
"Mousie dear? Are you there?"

Punch:

We anticipate what we loathe
or simmer. "Of what bonanza thinkest thou ill,
small smelly churl?" (Whack!)

The targets outnumber the marksmen. (Whack!)

This he is who, toothsome female? He who scuttles butts? (Whack!)
Is this the he of Cloudlet Eight where dreams are gratis, almost?
Who rang?

'Tis Low-Slung Hermal, pusher to the demi-monde. (Whack!)
"Drink & plough whomever you please. Ignore the cost
or may the devil do a hundred chin-ups,
taking moaning me in stride. It is many hours to infamy
& not quite time for din-din, my friend."
His mouth is much diminished.
He is otherwise our h&somest survivor.

Sump pumps pump however shallow the sentiment.

JUDY:

Out here in Nature I'm really really happy
in teensy tiny ways, wooo hooo!
Froggies in my panties!

Nothing makes me happier than peaceful buttered noodles,
the merest hint of companionship,
& thinking about—who else?—myself,
A Levantine doxy formerly, now a big, fat thought. I mean forever,
strangler.

Desire compounds the difference
especially on a pedestal. Can you hear me now?
How all my plans turn to l&fill? Be that as it may,
Project 31 ("Flemish Lint") is rolling right along,
donations are pouring in, lots of fabric, & I will sew until
my beating heart's humanitarian core is as content
as a chrysanthemum.

PUNCH:

& then? (I really meant "when?") (Whack!)
Flurry, blizzard, slush
& Dowl&, dead.
"Can we excuse our wrongs . . . ?"

The Legend of Chief Sequoia (He Makes Her Squeak)
Printemps!—renewed longings for that of which
one never gets enough, & above all else,
working well with others. (Whack!)

I am attractive, tell me your address,
I'll send you a merkin on & off.
Tell me your address, I'll send myself
at the end of the trail, trial, travails . . . a problem withal for
social engineering.
If you'd like to attend, please just be & leave it to me.
We'll remark how we differ.
In short, improvisation. (Whack!) Or perhaps
improvement.

Dan Tremaglio

H-1B Visa Expert Opinion Letter #0718

July 4, 2018

RE: Analysis of Positional Requirements for H-1B Visa Status

Position: Social Media Manager

Employer: Something Something Resorts Inc.

Candidate: Krishnahari, Jagganath

Dear Madam or Sir:

The purpose of this letter is in question. This will be made fully evident by the end, if it is not already.

In the meantime, the purpose of this letter is to provide an expert opinion in support of the H-1B Visa Application filed on behalf of Mr. Jagganath Krishnahari by Something Something Resorts Inc. for the position of Social Media Manager.

WAIT, WHAT?

An expert opinion letter. These are required as part of the H-1B Visa Application Process mandated by the Immigration & Nationality Act of 2017 Section 101(a)(15)(H) which allows U.S. employers to employ foreign workers in fulfillment of highly specialized positions.

WHICH BASICALLY MEANS:

Before a company like Something Something Resorts Inc. can employ a non-US citizen like Mr. Jagganath Krishnahari for a position like Social Media Manager, the company must first secure for him H-1B Visa Status. Here's how: the employer must provide, in addition to completed forms, fees, and battery of supportive documents, the written opinion of an expert in a field relevant to the position being offered, wherein the expert would opine that the candidate is indeed the ideal person for the position and that the position is specialized to a sufficient degree that it cannot be readily satisfied by an average pledge-of-allegiance-pledging US-of-A citizen.

INTRODUCTION & OVERVIEW

The following letter will provide an expert opinion in support of the H-1B Visa Application filed by Something Something Resorts Inc. on behalf of Mr. Jagganath Krishnahari by

a) discussing the credentials, experience, and expertise of the expert evaluator(s?) on no fewer than three narratorial planes

b) highlighting the genesis, goals, fears, triumphs, failures, and all-around corporate personhood of Something Something Resorts Inc.

c) outlining and analyzing the positional requirements and industry standards and expectations for the position of Social Media Manager

d) deriving the etymology, history, beliefs, academic and creative interests, ambitions, whims, and all-around human personhood of Mr. Jagganath Krishnahari before finally

e) concluding with an expertly rendered expert opinion and prophetic prognostication.

CREDENTIALS OF EXPERT OPINIONATOR

Expert opinion letters customarily commence with a subsection designed to assure any official application evaluator that the author of this expert opinion letter is in fact an expert with the requisite educational and experiential credentials and that the next 10, 25, or in some cases 49 pages will warrant their legitimate professional consideration.

"I"

I am the one writing this, but am I really the expert? Let me put it this way: I am the letter's author but not its signatory. Why? Because I earn a competitive but by no means elite income writing expert opinion letters on behalf of experts who ostensibly write them on behalf of employers who ostensibly write them on behalf of candidates who ostensibly do not have a job yet. I presume to be doing good work. Or at least doing no harm. I have been doing/not doing it since 2017 when the aforementioned legislation was signed into law by the United States Congress.

AN EXPERT OPINION GHOST WRITER???

Exactly. Before that I worked in a bookstore on Long Island, a job I was astonished to loathe. Seriously, did not see that coming. I always thought such a position would allow one to sit around and read all day and feed smelly cats and perhaps occasionally debate some wiseass about a text that sucks but is considered magnificent or vice versa,

but the truth is I never once got to read on the job, nor did I ever get to fill out one of those EMPLOYEE PICKS cards you see taped to shelves, which is the only type of paperwork I have ever aspired to. The reason why is my boss, Donald, was sub-admirable. We used to call him Donald Dick in a duck voice behind his back, which was almost funny and the highlight of that craphouse job. So when I finally got this H-1B ghosting gig I was pleased because it pays five times as much which is still not a ton in the grand scheme of things but it felt great, a least for a while, or for about three months, which is when my student loan company got wind of the salary bump and increased my income-based repayment plan accordingly. But enough about me.

CREDENTIALS OF ACTUAL EXPERT WHOSE OPINION IS BEING GHOSTED

Doctor E. Pancake earned a double PhD in Creative Writing and Political Science from Eastern Assurbanipal University where he now teaches and therefore understands better than most how Fiction and Politics are pretty much the same subject, both concerning the ability of an author/authority to convince large swaths of the population that what is obviously unreal is in fact reality. Think about it. Pick up a novel and note the word FICTION right there on the back cover and yet from the first sentence on, every word, every comma, every image is carefully elected to make you forget that fact, elected to make you think it's real, elected to make you feel it's real. Literature tells us, *Get ready? I'm going to lie to your face now*, and then lies to our faces for days, for weeks, until finally it stops and says, *Wait, did I just lie to you? I'm not sure anymore. What do you think*? This suspension of disbelief makes not only the story-world possible but the world in which the story-world is possible

possible. Ponder the implications of this with regard to the State, God, the Self, etc. Doctor E. Pancake ponders and thereby comprehends expertly the ins and out of Social Media Management which resides at a natural confluence of these fields. Here he is in his own excruciating templated words which end up cut-and-pasted into every single expert opinion letter he allegedly authors (only not today, for today I am drinking on the job, if a little heavier than normal, in keeping with Friday afternoon Manhattan mores):

CREDENTIALS OF ACTUAL EXPERT OPINIONATOR (IN CHARACTER)

I am providing this expert opinion letter and positional analysis based on my educational background in Advertising, Creative Writing (Fiction), Web Marketing, Web Design, Economics, Political Science, and related areas; my experience as a university professor in Advertising, Creative Writing (Fiction), Web Marketing, Web Design, Economics, Political Science, and related subjects; my industry experience in Advertising, Creative Writing (Fiction), Web Marketing, Web Design, Economics, Political Science, and related subjects; and my expertise and experience as an evaluator of academic credentials, professional experience, positions of employment, and industrial norms in Advertising, Creative Writing (Fiction), Web Marketing, Web Design, Economics, Political Science, and related areas. I am in a position to provide opinion based on my personal background, educationally and professionally, in Advertising, Creative Writing (Fiction), Web Marketing, Web Design, Economics, Political Science, and related areas. In the past, I have offered expert opinion letters and analyses of the academic and professional credentials of candidates for university admissions and employment positions in Advertising, Creative Writing (Fiction), Web Marketing, Web

Design, Economics, Political Science, and related areas. I've had an opportunity to observe and compare the abilities of numerous talented students in the field of Advertising, Creative Writing (Fiction), Web Marketing, Web Design, Economics, Political Science, and related fields, and to analyze the ways in which the educational backgrounds of the students have been applied in professional industry. Additionally, I have become intimately familiar with the nature and depth of knowledge and skill, both theoretical and practical, gained by university students who study Advertising, Creative Writing (Fiction), Web Marketing, Web Design, Economics, Political Science, and related subjects, and how that knowledge and skill is recruited and applied by employers in a variety of industries. Thus, I believe that I am qualified to opine on positions of employment in the areas of Advertising, Creative Writing (Fiction), Web Marketing, Web Design, Economics, Political Science, and related areas as offered by Something Something Resorts Inc. to Mr. Jagganath Krishnahari.

To further elaborate, I am providing this expert opinion letter and position evaluation based on my experience as a professor and evaluator of academic experience credentials at Eastern Assurbanipal University in Moab, Connecticut. I am providing this expertise letter and positional analysis based on my experience as a professor and evaluator of foreign academic experience credentials for university admissions and submission to the US Citizenship and Immigration Services. I am a tenured professor and a chairperson of the department of—

OK ENOUGH—YOU GET THE POINT

Sorry but you had to experience that firsthand. Otherwise you would never understand what I am up to here. Have you every read anything more profoundly redundant, more intentionally un-readable, a more inimical assault on the vitality of the present? The above subsection would typically continue for no fewer than five pages. You understand now how redundancy has been weaponized. Write formally, write intelligently, but write slowly, soullessly and without surprise, thereby forcing readers to either skim ahead or lose consciousness, their cross-eyed faces crashing atop the keyboard.

A FEW SNAP TAKEAWAYS

1.) The devil is not in the details but indices.

2.) Lucifer is monolingual & speaks legalese.

3.) Little Nicky is a technical writer in an ill-lit office in New York who inhabits the cubicle nearest the shitter.

4.) The made-up statistic that 96.66% of all legislation is signed by men who have not read the legislation is not a made-up statistic.

5.) Speak clearly & predictably & tediously & the cops will go away. This is how to talk when you've got a body in the trunk.

BUT NO MORE!!!

If you're still reading this, it is because I am correct in my thinking and will soon be unemployed. If not, I'll simply have to try again come Monday. This is my great experiment, America!

I AM ALSO DRUNK . . .

This should be stated bluntly. It's 2:40 PM on a Friday in Manhattan and I would be the pariah not to be. Yet we persist.

INTRODUCTION OF EMPLOYER

Something Something Resorts Inc. (hereafter Something, he, or him) was born as Something Something Company in Albany, New York in 1945. A precocious child, his primary school teachers had this to say of him:

> "A delight to direct. He devours knowledge as ravenously as unrenewable resources."

> "By far the most likely to succeed in the class . . . a true cut-throat professional."

> "Capable of excusing any wretched interaction with the words, 'Hey, nothing personal, it's just business.'"

On his 13th birthday Something stood an imposing 6'9" and weighed a healthy $7.5 million. Here entered his first vision of what he could become: a multinational corporation. His greatest desire: MORE. His greatest fear: not getting his greatest desire. His most admirable quality: a willingness to work hard, which is to say sacrifice, which is to say to trade what he has for what he hasn't. In those early days he had just sixteen pairs of hands and worked every one of them blistered and bloody. Not once did he sleep for more than four hours in a night. He averaged two. While others dreamed, he diversified. Early ventures into residential real estate quickly expanded into the commercial sector and public utilities as well as energy, entertainment, mining, the auto industry, and publishing. Every investment was vastly profitable. He didn't defeat competitors, he bought them out. He grew and grew and grew and grew like a cash-colored algae bloom in a hot rising sea. By age 30 Something crossed the one hundred million mark and didn't look back. Ten years later not just one but two zeros had latched sucker-fish-like onto his combined net worth.

Only then did Something pause to reflect. He looked out at all he had made and he saw that it was good. A market lay at his feet. Was this a happy time? Yes, he decided, it was. He was not the biggest company but he was in the biggest league. Here began a season of contentment for Something. He grew a beard. His founding father begat with a woman an heir and then a girl. The kids came of age in marble offices, playing catch with staplers. They shouted their first imperatives into wireless headsets. Receptionists laughed. Every employee went about buoyant and smiling. Something was a company every college man dreamed of being hired by on graduation day and retiring from fifty years later. Wages and profits were like a sprinter's legs, equal length, equal speed, keeping record breaking pace. Bonuses came on Christmas Eve. A golden age.

Then the founding father dropped dead lining up a putt on the 17th green. Stroke. The chief executor position passed on to the elder heir who had visions of his own. This was the day of dot com. Money was in the air now, in invisible waves, a see-through ghost that still cast a shadow. Never before had value been so abstract, so reputed. Until then industry had been about hardware and infrastructure and property. Now it would be about information, intelligence, narrative, myth. Reality itself was a new world waiting to be staked. What this meant for Something was this: the resorts sector of his empire took center stage. He carved his big beard into a sleek goatee. Assets were sold off and siphoned into beachside getaways and cruise lines and golf courses and casinos with infinity pools atop towers in the clouds. What is a resort, after all, but an alternate reality, a refuge from reason.

Did his scheme work? Yup. Something's net worth tripled within three years, a historic run. Until it went bankrupt overnight, a historic flop. He managed to consolidate and rebound and a few years later had recovered most of his peak worth before losing it all a second time. The heir was bought out. Something recovered under new management and was sold again before going bankrupt a third time. He allegedly recovered once more, though no one knows exactly how or what his actual worth is today. What we do know is he's looking for a new Social Media Manager for the southeastern coastal sector and has identified Mr. Jagganath Krishnahari as the right man for the job.

THE POSITION IN BRIEF

The quintessential Social Media Manager means to make every event an EVENT! What happens HERE should be known about EVERYWHERE! Capital letters are ENCOURAGED! So are exclamation marks!!!!!!! The best Social Media Manager seeks to stamp the BRAND across every ray of light! This is his method: each post and photo and status update must amount to an ACCUSATION, an INDICTMENT on the head of every reader and viewer and listener that they ARE MISSING OUT, that by not being present they are EXCLUDED, they are OTHERIZED, they are LOSERS!!! Even if the event has not happened yet, the ideal Social Media Manager must makes the public UTTERLY TERRIFIED to miss it! The public must not be convinced but COMPELLED!

INDUSTRY ANALYSIS OF POSITION

The position of Social Media Manager is an entry level position yet highly specialized and requires both thinking abilities and doing abilities at an above average level and cannot possibly be performed by a person with less than a Bachelor's Degree in the field of Literature, Philosophy, Anthropology, Psychology, Web Marketing, Advertising, Macroeconomics, Political Science, Art, or some closely related field, which is to say a Bachelor's Degree in absolutely anything whatsoever. Furthermore, the ideal candidate for the position of Social Media Manager should over-caffeinate and say "like" like a real lot.

However, an expert analysis of the industry quickly reveals that candidates of this feather are more difficult to come by than it might initially seem. Eligible candidates typically to go into fields like Journalism, Academia, Poetry, Organic Subsistence Farming, Heavy Drug Use and/or Drop Out of Society Completely. The best are the Drop-outs but Drop-outs cannot typically be convinced to take jobs in grocery stores let alone multi-national corporations like Something Something Resorts Inc. Hence the H-1B option and Mr. Jagganath Krishnahari . . .

INTRODUCTION OF CANDIDATE

Mr. Jagganath Krishnahari grew up in the post-colonized city of Puri, India where the English word "juggernaut" was coined by British writer Sir John Mandeville in 1357. In his travel memoir, Mandeville describes a religious procession where an enormous wooden wheelhouse—which locals seem to refer to as Jagganath—is paraded down the streets while the faithful toss themselves before it to be crushed. Hence the English usage:

> **jug·ger·naut** : *noun* 1. a huge, destructive, unstoppable force or institution. 2. anything requiring blind devotion or cruel sacrifice

Mr. Jagganath Krishnahari, candidate for the position of Social Media Manager being offered by Something Something Resorts Inc., laughs a little whenever he hears this word in everyday speech. To begin with, he knows no one has ever thrown themselves sacrificially before the wheelhouse paraded each year through his birth city's streets.

More than that, he is tickled to think how markedly un-juggernaut-like the deity Jagganath is in person. Sir John Mandeville, surely bewildered and overheated, confused the massive wheelhouse for the tiny murti or statue atop it. Far from terrifying, the actual Jagganath can be described as a small wooden stump with a smiley face painted across it. Two round white eyes with black pupils stare out over a swooping scarlet grin. There are many stories about the origin of Jagganath's curious appearance and one of them goes like this:

"NO PEEKING IN PURI"

Long ago the inhabitants of Puri wished to build a temple but could not afford the murti that would be its centerpiece. Then one day a really really old brahman came to the city and said he was in fact a murti-maker who would gladly provide them his service in exchange for room and board. The town was skeptical, for this man appeared exceedingly old and frail. Would he even survive the job? Ultimately though they had little choice and said okay, deal. The brahman had the tools he needed. All he asked was that a curtain be stretched across the sanctum while he worked and that nobody glimpse beneath it until he finished. No peeking, he insisted. Everybody agreed. The curtain was stretched and he got to work. For several days the sound of sawing and hammering and chiseling and miscellaneous murti-making could be heard from behind the curtain. Then all fell silent. One week passed. Then a second. Everyone worried. An ancient guy died in the temple. Now he's rotting in there. Surely that's bad luck. We need to get him out asap. So they lifted the curtain and the old brahman turned and said I told you no peeking! He vanished, leaving the murti unfinished. The citizens of Puri were sad and embarrassed but soon fell in love with their inchoate godhead, his woodblock body and elemental glee, his two stubs for arms.

INTRODUCTION OF CANDIDATE, CONT'D

Mr. Jagganath Krishnahari, named after his birth city's beloved deity, came of age under the monumental pressure to learn the language that so comically misappropriates their name. For Mr. Jagganath Krishnahari, English was not a language but a currency that guaranteed upward mobility. He pretended to be Christian in order to study it at a convent school or he mostly pretended. He was not formally religious but was also unsure what that really meant, to be formally religious. He believed in all gods and he believed in none of them.

This changed during his Masters work at the University of Benares when he began administering fulltime to logos. He always felt language was power but now he saw it as a power that could be taken up and aimed rather than merely learned and obeyed. English wasn't just a ticket out of Puri, it was his name on that ticket, his candidacy on the global market. He applied to half a dozen doctoral programs in Great Britain, America, and Canada. He was hoping for an American school but in the end the University of Toronto offered him the best deal and so he bought a Blue Jays cap and looked out for Michael Ondaatje and wrote a dissertation reexamining post-colonial Straussian interpretations of the Mahabharata in light of computer stylistic analyses that suggest heavy Vedic influence on early Ancient Greek Philosophy in general and Plato in particular.

Upon graduation he decided he didn't want a job in academia just yet. What he really wanted was to focus on his own myth-making for a while and started looking for jobs in America that would get him a work visa but not require much effort. He happened upon a Social Media Management position without knowing exactly what such a position entailed and sent out an application.

SUITABILITY OF CANDIDATE TO HANDLE POSITION

In order to handle the position of Social Media Manager being offered by Something Something Resorts Inc., a candidate must have completed prior to recruitment a Bachelors degree in Literature, Philosophy, Anthropology, Psychology, Web Marketing, Advertising, Macroeconomics, Political Science, Art, or some closely related field. I, Doctor E. Pancake, am an expert in the fields of Literature, Philosophy, Anthropology, Psychology, Web Marketing, Advertising, Macroeconomics, Political Science, Art, and several closely related fields and have reviewed the academic credentials of the candidate for the position of Social Media Manager being offered by Something Something Resorts Inc. and have determined that Mr. Jagganath Krishnahari has completed a suitable analytical academic background in the aforementioned areas and is qualified to handle the requisite job duties associated with the position.

TERMS OF EMPLOYMENT

Visa duration: eleven months (unless it lasts longer (or less))

Candidate will be paid: USD (but not enough to stick around for)

Benefits: ha, good one

Health care coverage: ha ha, another good one

HOW I SEE THIS PANNING OUT

I am not the expert but I am writing this letter and I say Mr. Jagganath Krishnahari appears too thoughtful for the position of Social Media Manager for a company like Something Something Resorts. I therefore predict he will thrive at it. He'll be like a master sword-maker who inherits a bakery from an eccentric uncle and kills it at cake making. Or like a gynecologist who falls pleasantly into a penchant for urban planning. He'll be odd but original and buzz worthy. The playing field will promptly warp around him. And he will hate it. Obviously. I don't see him drinking on the job but I do see him becoming more confident and speaking his mind more and more bluntly to his so-called supervisors. He won't be fired, he'll leave on his own accord before his visa expires, entering that purgatorial grey area. He'll gain access to an electric car. I don't know how but he will. Inheritance? Mild charlatanry? Whatever. I prophesy he will become a driver and start vlogging from behind the wheel as he moves from city to city, composing an oral epic of the massacre of language that is America today. Two years after that he'll accept an associate professorship. Two years after that his first novel will appear, a work of autofiction entitled *The Travels of Sir John Mandeville*.

CONCLUSION

The purpose of this letter was to provide an expert opinion in support of the H-1B Visa application filed on behalf of Mr. Jagganath Krishnahari by Something Something Resorts Inc. for the position of Social Media Manager.

Did I do that?

This expert opinion letter will likely be my last. I do not foresee employment with my current employer perpetuating past Monday. This letter was due at noon today and now it is 6 PM and I am leaving. Writing these things was not so bad. Sometimes I'd get attached to a candidate despite the strangled format. The details of a hometown, a degree, a single aspiration or two would add up to an actual person. Know what's weird? We ghosts never find out if a letter is successful or not. For the last year I've been writing fifteen to twenty of these a week and never once heard what comes of them. We never learn if a candidate was hired or how he faired on the job. This is the life of an expert opinion ghost writer. How many other fields have to deal with not knowing whether one way of doing their thing is better than another, with not knowing if a character's career veered one way on account of your depiction of it or veered another? Reminds me of shouting into a deep cave, waiting for an echo to return.

Still Waiting,

Doctor E. Pancake
Professor and Chairperson
Departments of Creative Writing and Political Science
Eastern Assurbanipal University

Julia Drescher

6 from "our office our offense"

(1)

With neither purpose nor dignity : a substance

Cunt is a concept & a distance
Its etymological slur its constant

Gut by gut a ruminant
Cunt loves a plant & a star

On the undersurface of leaves : how it breathes, how it eats
Soil, sunlight, intoxicants

Capable of intent & romance
Acacia enlists

"Is it really nothing but reflex & coincidence?"
A dusk & a fragrance, the cant of physics

With blasphemy's sweetness, viciously
With evil phonemes falling consistently

Love speaks its reciprocity
Having not yet lived

It scientifically thickens
It is a mood so it is a style

Cut mint swung letter & some spit
On the philosophy of it

It is content to list :
A flank of anything, a fool for pigeons, a hoof of touching

In this immediacy & nearness
In this pregnant paucity

With this small vocabulary & without profundity, but with viscosity
Its slither its slew & spoke warm bend—

Trees would leap, birds would break
& cellulose is the base

Flowing from afar, nurturing the stars, whatever
With affective textures

The bodily winds

(3)

Monosyllabically thick
It comes
A hellish transom

Nothing surprises language
Or cunts
Grammatically

As event & as context
A lapse of years & trenches, this distance

In obscurity unending
In contingency's tense
Lounging & laughing

& laughing
Without & full of gravity
Deliberately feint & couching since

The 17th century obscenely
Quaint when it's alone

Honing the predictive functions : a fleshy a rose a vulgar a tongue
A tendency
"To become a woman, a contemplative person"

It rhymes with vital
Epistemologically

(4)

A picture's prosability
Lumps of dust

& paper full of molds & ridges especially
Obsessed with cityedge & debris

Intricately a rose a rubbish heap
With discursive capacities

Lavishly the trash of syntax walking

Small & fast & large & vast & middling
An armature & a weight

Categorically a poor brocade
A table breaks the context

Bleeds—the new latin derived from ancient greek—
Becoming linguistically
The good bad earth

Fundamentally fern
An ambulacral grove

The extra that senses the season

(5)

With the pungency of cut beets
The longform squirrel

Guttural flashings
With heat & apparatuses

With botanical curve & clutch
It verves the egg's engine

& licks the louvre off
A scribble a scallop

A pain & a pony laughing
When particle men

& perception does a lot of talking

(6)

Where the crook in an arm begins

Half dead end as half continuance
The double-bird experience
Half cul-de-sac half park
The disk of the body is dusk, the dusk of the body is viscera

It feels like a portal but people live here

Jack Foley

Canine

You know very well we can't do that today, said Jessica.

Arf said the dog.

Besides, I think they're closed.

Arf arf said the dog.

You checked on the Internet said Jessica.

Arf said the dog.

I know you enjoy Vietnamese food. Especially pho.

Arf ARF said the dog.

You handled the chopsticks particularly well.

Arf arf arf arf arf.

Yes I know it's an old family tradition. You were taught when you were just a pup.

Arf arffff.

Yes, you do handle them better than I do. Especially when you use your tail.

Arf hah said the dog.

Well, all right.

Hah hah hah said the dog.

So they went to the Vietnamese restaurant and had a very nice meal.

Afterwards the dog said Arf. It was larrupin'.

Jessica walked him over to the fire hydrant, where he relieved himself.

Jessica discovered she could understand Doggish about a year ago. She had no idea how it had happened but suddenly everything the dog said was intelligible to her though it was not to anyone else.

She lived alone and had few friends so the dog was a wonderful companion to her. Sometimes they would have long philosophical discussions. She discovered that the dog was not only well bred but well read, though he did not read in the usual fashion: he read by chewing the book. He had devoured many pages of many diverse books in this way and, though entirely self educated, had quite a range of knowledge. At times she complained about his use of foreign terms. Heidegger was bad enough but Derrida? Not to mention Aristotle and Plato in the original Greek. He especially enjoyed barking the opening lines of the Iliad. Once he growled, "We see TO KALON decreed in the marketplace." She told him she liked the music of what he recited but didn't understand a word. When they walked together it was understood that she was on the leash, not he. She complained when he sniffed the genitalia of female dogs but he explained that he was after all a dog and had to lead a dog's life: certain behaviors were expected, *de rigeur*.

One night, after a particularly heated discussion, he told her that according to Freudian theory she would probably be considered completely wacko. Talking to a dog was one thing but understanding a dog as well? Who would believe her? Did she know that there were dogs who had considerable knowledge of all the sciences and arts but who, because they were dogs, could not be heard. Often they were far more intelligent than their so called "masters," but things being as they were they had to disguise their superior intellects and put on the false face of bow wow and tail wagging just as some humans had to bow and scrape and say, "Yessir." There was no way for them to advance in any profession. The lowest of the low would be hired before them. And think of dog years! he went on. Seven of yours make one of ours. And they say that our first year is equal to fifteen of yours. There are many odes and laments unknown to humans but widely disseminated among the canine tribes.

"Let the bone you bury
Remind you
Of the briefness of life
You too will be a bone in the dust someday.
As leaves in autumn are the years of the canine.
Copulate as you may, dear stud
Make the sweet pup.
He too will feel the lash of the leash
He too will howl his days
And fall to the bitter jaws.
Brief is the warp and brief the woof.
Woof."

As he spoke he began to whimper. Jessica put her hand to his paw and sighed as he slowly wagged his tail.

One day the dog told her he wished to go out for a walk—alone. He needed, he said, "a little space."

"Of course," said Jessica in an understanding tone.

"Arf," he said appreciatively.

But he was gone for hours and she began to worry. The day turned to night and she worried more. She blew on the dog whistle which she knew only his sensitive ears might hear. There was no answer. Where could he be?

Days passed. She went out to look for him. Perhaps he had been attacked by some animal or other—perhaps even another dog. She scoured the neighborhood, put ads in the local papers, went to the Internet. No response.

Then one day, after a week had passed, there was a scratching at the door. It was he!

Arf, he said passively as she reached out to embrace him.

"Where have you been," she said. "I've been worried sick."

"I'm sorry to have troubled you," he answered. "I've been—away."

"Away?"

"Yes. During this week when I have had to stand on my own four feet, I have reached deeply into myself. I have sought to find the dogsoul that drives me, that drives my dogsbody."

"And did you find it?"

"I believe so, yes. I have found the secret that I have tried to avoid my whole dog's life long. It is called wildness. There, out in the world, entirely on my own, relying on no one for food and service, I met a stray bitch. At first we regarded each other with suspicion as we sniffed in dog greeting. But something about her scent intoxicated me—poisoned me but thrilled me. I realized suddenly that my ancestors—and hers—were wolves. Not man's (or woman's) best friend but wild creatures who were unto themselves and not beholden to anyone. I thrilled to the thought. Sire and dam; to whelp. I had grown too accustomed to the amenities you offered me. I had grown too bookish. I needed to break free, to undo the leash—the umbilical cord. You have been kind to me and I am grateful. You have brought me into the light, but in doing so you have made me forget the dark. You have made me forget myself. This bitch reminded me of the furious—I would almost say divine—creature I was and could be again. I want—raw flesh not dog meat."

"But what—what of us," said Jessica. "Does all we have been to one another mean nothing to you? What of our"—she hesitated—"love?"

"You have been my mistress, and you have been a good mistress: but I need a mate. I need the freshness of the stars above me and the air. Above all, I need to kill. I will never forget you. I promise you that. But I can no longer be in your world. Adieu, adieu. You will hear me when the moon is bright, when the air carries my cry to you. Remember me. Ah! Ah! Où sont les hurlements d'antan!"

He finished and turned away, his tail moving softly as he began to gather speed. Into the night.

Jessica stood in the doorway and watched. She began to weep. And then she began to howl. The air carried her cries as far as it could—and then they vanished.

For a while she could detect his scent, but then it was gone.

She bit her hand fiercely till the blood came.

Woof.

She would follow him into the night. She would get him back. She tasted the blood that flowed from her hand. All of her senses glowed. She would murder the bitch that took him from her. She tore off her clothes and felt the fur between her legs. Moonlight was in the window and beckoned. "I am no longer . . . human."

acnektilcolcowhklpoipqlvlyliprqppkmc
woofarfwoofarfbowwowwoofarfarfarf
woofarfbowarfwoofwoofWOOF
bowwowwowgrrrrrrwoofarfwoof
bowwoofwowgrrrrrrahoooooarfwoof
rrrrrrrrrrrrrrwoofarfarfwowwobrrr
woofrrrhahhahhahhah (wag tail at this point)
awoooooo
brrrrrrffffffffbowwowhahhahhahwoofarf!

CORINA BARDOFF

THE QUELLERS OF THE FLOOD

I parked in the spot designated for women visiting the witches, beneath the sign with the image of a grackle. I started off on the path and turned right at the pile of six stones, as the instructions online directed, taking off my flip-flops when they got stuck in the mud. Great trees had fallen in last night's storm. The witches live in a maintenance shed in a large city park, and I arrived barefoot, with red mud wrapped around my feet like a spa treatment. A park worker in a green uniform was loading piles of fodder onto a truck.

"Are you a witch?" I asked.

"I take care of the animals in the petting zoo," the park worker said. "I can see that you need help." A witch came out then, squinting in the sunlight and carrying two sacks of grain. She looked me up and down.

"Take this to the chickens. We're running out of space in there," she said to the park worker. "Hose your feet off," she said to me, "and then come on in."

I used to like my problems, but now I dislike them. I know the location of every speck of dirt in my house, and feel it throbbing like a dying firefly. I feel the reproach of my leftovers sitting in Styrofoam. Last night's storm snapped old live oaks, flooded the Trinity River, and downed power lines. In some storms, I have felt enveloped by the supercell, soothed by thunder. In some storms, I have felt electrified, communicative, and rational like a math problem. In this storm, which lasted all night and got the tornado warnings whining, I felt snapped, flooded, and downed. My dog Rhubarb hopped into the bathtub and looked at me reproachfully when I came for her. I sat on the cold tiles, chilled by the air conditioning, counting how many miles away the storm was by counting the seconds between lightning strikes and thunder claps. It receded, approached again, backed off, and came nearer, crashing over me again and again like an ocean. It was slaying me. I am slain. I went to the witches so they could reorganize my emotions.

"Stop getting pedicures," said one witch. "How can anything escape your body? You're suffocating it. Paint your fingernails black and don't let them chip. Then leave your toenails clean. Have a seat."

I sat on a wicker stool. It was a large maintenance shed. I wondered if the witches were sisters or married or just business partners. Both were in their forties, I thought, tall, slim, with pale blond hair and black nail polish. The one who spoke to me had dark brown eyes encircled by smoldering eyeliner. The other had blue eyes and seemed sleepy.

"What's your name and when were you born?" asked the sleepy witch.

My name is Carnation and I was born October 26, 1986.

The dark-eyed witch stiffened. "Carnation, honey, listen: if you want your children to have ordinary problems give them ordinary names. If you want your children to have rare, complicated problems, name them something rare."

"Which is better?"

The light-eyed witch shook her head. "But carnations are such common, cheap flowers," she said. "What I want to know is: are you a red carnation, a pink carnation, or a white carnation?"

"I always liked the ones that are dyed different colors like blue and green."

The witches looked at me in disgust.

"What about good things?" I asked. "How do you name your child if you want her to have rare, good emotions?"

"Carnation sweetie," said the dark-eyed witch. "Good things are hard to control. It's easier to prevent bad things. Good things are more like accidents or noise."

"Carnation darling, why did you come to us?" said the light-eyed witch. "You are not here to ask for good things. You are here because of a problem."

I told them I felt snapped, flooded, and downed. I feel full of sugar like a hangover. The whole world says, "Oh, Carnation," and I say "What? What?" There are a million precious animals that live inside my body and all of them are drowning in a terrible flood.

There was a sword hanging on the wall of the shed. It looked so heavy, I felt like I was lifting it with my eyes.

"Don't worry about that, Carnation sweetie," said the light-eyed witch. "That's not for you."

"Who's it for?"

"You know where we are," said the light-eyed witch. "We're in a state of Southern Baptists who remember the Alamo. Sometimes our neighbors who aren't mockingbirds and foxes get a little upset about witches in their public parks."

The witch continued. "Some people need more money. Their health is bad. They need someone to realize they would be perfect together. They need custody of their children. Their car is broken. Their cat has run away. Their son is struggling in school and has stopped speaking to them. Their partner is abusive. Their family back home is suffering. You are neither sick nor mentally ill. And yet you are in distress. Something inside you is incorrect and yet you are listening to it. I don't know if this is rare, but it is not a problem that people come to see witches for very often. People usually come because they want something or want something to stop. What do you even want?"

My name, to me, is the soft, vulnerable self-hood that sits alongside my kidneys. Rhubarb, do you have rare canine problems? Wolves, coyotes, dingoes without names must not have problems at all besides finding food and a mate. Are names problems that humans give to the animals they love?

When I got home, Rhubarb smelled my bag carefully. She stopped, her tail mid-wag, sat without my telling her to, and waited. "Let's go outside, Rhubarbie," I sang to her, and she followed me out. While she sniffed around the yard, I snuck back in and locked the door. She can open the door if it's unlocked.

In the bathroom, I took the vial of Magic Mold that the witches had given me out of my bag. They told me I was weak, and it would give me strength.

I want the world to be all birds' nests and pebbles. That's impossible. There are conference rooms, cruise ships, and concrete. That ivy isn't native and it's undermining the building's structure.

The opposite of snapped is straight and whole and tall.

The opposite of flooded is dry.

The opposite of downed is lifted, carried, sailing.

If our world is the cheese, the Magic Mold is the partly cloudy sky: blue sky that makes your insides constrict with repulsion. As instructed, I dipped my finger into the mold, shivering, and rubbed it into my bellybutton and both of my ears.

I removed my toenail polish. When I heard Rhubarb pawing at the back door, I went out to the living room and saw her through the glass looking alert and worried. The taste of the mold penetrated through my ears, into my sinuses, and down my throat: old hazelnuts, shiitake, and Advil if you chew it. The mold's fuzziness crept into my stomach like a time-lapse vine.

I let Rhubarb back into the house and she pressed her nose into my still-exposed bellybutton, and took two deep, suspicious sniffs before I was able to shove her away. She scampered off to the bedroom.

I was beginning to feel strong. I felt my core in a Pilates clench. I wanted to get into a fistfight but with my abs instead of my hands. My esophagus felt caked with mud. The hair on my head rose with static electricity.

Rhubarb walked back in on her two hind legs, her forepaws dangling foppishly. She looked at me ecstatically, like, "Isn't this what you always wanted'?! Now we can dance!"

I clenched my abs tighter. I am a bundle of sticks. Nothing can break me. I made a sign on poster board that said, "No, thanks!" in black letters and hung it on my front door.

I felt like my joints would never bend again, even as I bent them. The specks of dirt in my house did not exist, had never existed, and anyway, this house was me: each room was created anew as I walked into it. I felt a stillness not of inertia but of power. My phone rang. I picked it up automatically, laughed like a grackle, and then hung up. I turned it off completely.

I was proud of all my objects now. The TV that I had anguished over in Best Buy, the garage sale lamp, my feeble display of crystals: what a good collector of things I was. My several succulents were thriving all thanks to my genius with things that are alive. My eyes were dry and burning, and my throat was so parched, I knew I could barely speak if I wanted to (I did not). My insides were dry. My stomach had no juices, and instead of using acid to process food, was compressing it into perfect, dense cubes like at a municipal dump.

I felt, though proud and unbreakable, also like a wrung-out sponge. I worried about Rhubarb, who was following me around the house, still on her hind paws, furiously wagging her tail and panting heavily. Her little back legs were shaking.

"Good girl," I tried. I held a bowl of water in front of her face and she drank standing. I poured myself some iced tea and painted my nails black. Nothing can get inside of me.

I sat on the couch, though I felt like standing on it. I patted a cushion. "Up up, Rhubarbie!" Rhubarb likes being on the couch, and I thought it might calm her down. She looked tempted but unsure of how to jump from her upright position. I lifted her, but she tried to stand on the couch, teetered, and fell onto the floor. She twisted around so much, I thought she might break her back, but she wobbled to her hind legs again, wagging her tail sheepishly, and began to walk. Her legs shook, and she was crying, a high-pitched, mournful whine, interrupted by pathetic little woofs.

I am tremendous. I am an arid expanse so large I can be seen from space. But I am only a pothole filling with water without my dog. Rhubarb had taken medicine not prescribed to her, and I had to find an antidote.

"Let's go for a ride, puppy!"

It was storming again, a violent, luscious pouring and thundering, but I am Death Valley. I carried Rhubarb to the car, put her in the front seat, and buckled her in sitting up like a small child. I did not drive to the witches. I imagined they would chastise me for allowing harm to come to an animal. Worse, I imagined they wouldn't care about Rhubarb at all.

I drove cautiously through the rain, tensed, the steering wheel becoming a part of my body. It was Saturday and most people were huddled inside. I was hoping to stumble upon a trope: a magical store that appears when you need it, that you can't find again when you retrace your steps.

Carnation sugar, you should have known: magical shops are for the beginning of stories. They don't exist in new, sprawling cities like this one, and you can't reach them in a car.

The rain came horizontally in the wind. An American flag the size of a swimming pool twisted and thrashed and fought for its country above a Denny's. A mega-church sat with empty acres of parking spaces. Everywhere I looked, stores were closed; their employees couldn't get to work because trees fell on their cars; the strip malls flooded; the power went out and the ice cream melted. Sections of freeway were closed. Is it ridiculous to have a problem of your own amid all this destruction?

A parking lot fortified by light, the LEDs battling against the siege of storm. I felt all the tiny animals that live within the desert of my body peer out, wondering if the coast was clear. Not quite, my kangaroo rats, my beautiful iguanas, my darkling beetles. But there is hope. The Walmart Supercenter is open.

Rhubarb and I walked in each on our two hind legs. The greeter looked at us in astonishment.

"She's a service dog," I said. Rhubarb teetered and whined.

"Can I help you find anything?" asked the greeter.

"No, thanks!" I said. "She's all the help I need!"

Rhubarb sniffed the air, the desert animals within me sniffed the air, and I took a blue basket from the stack. Coyote, burrowing owl, Rhubarb, where should we go? We stepped into the forest of aisles.

Of course, they led me to the pet department. The beginning of it shimmered with the bubbling of tanks and the hustling of little fish. Beyond the tanks were toys shaped like mice and birds, balls that squeak, and pots of growing catnip. Then we came to the feed section, heavy with tinned cat food, sacks of rabbit kibble, and dog chow. I heard a sweet, sad "chree, chree, chree." It came from a brown sparrow hopping unsteadily on top of a bag of seeds for cockatiels.

"Oh, hello, little friend." Rhubarb wagged her tail, almost knocking herself off balance.

"Chree, chree, chree."

"Are you trapped, little sparrow?" There were no people around, and anyway there is no shame in talking to animals in distress.

"Chree chree."

"You can ride on my shopping basket and I'll lead you out." The sparrow seemed to have a skeptical look in its black eyes.

"Chree chree chree." It pecked at the thick industrial plastic of the seed sack below it.

"Oh, you're hungry." It blinked at me. I reached into my purse and pulled out the Swiss army knife on my key chain. The sparrow hopped back and I sliced the bag six inches; it opened like a wound. The sparrow hopped into it and pecked intently at the millet and pumpkin seeds. Rhubarb stepped forward to sniff the bag, which was on a shelf just above her nose. The sparrow chirped happily, I thought, and flew to perch on my basket, chirped again, and then flew away. We followed. He led us deeper into the pet department, past hamster wheels and straw, before alighting on a blue sign advertising Everyday Low Prices.

"Chirp chirp." He flew back toward the seeds. Rhubarb and I were left in an aisle of bones: of pigs' ears, smoked knuckles, monster elk antlers,

and lamb trotters. I felt uneasy and brittle. My desert creatures burrowed into my pelvis to hide. Rhubarb whined nervously and then began shout-barking at the shelves. To my horror, I saw two human eyes looking at us. There was a face among the bones. There was a man hiding between the shelves. A scream rose from the animals in my pelvis, but dissipated weakly in my vocal cords. My abs clenched tighter.

"What the hell is wrong with your dog?" asked the man in the shelves. His voice felt like sandpaper on my ears.

"What the hell are you doing in there?"

"Now, what does it look like I'm doing here, young lady?"

I am a furious sandstorm walking through the Walmart. Do not call me "young lady."

"Waiting to scare people."

"Well, I'm waiting. It's true. I'm waiting for the store to close."

"And what will you do when the store closes?"

"Eat some apples and peanut butter, and then go pick some nice blankets in the bedding department and sleep."

"You live here?"

"I stay here sometimes. You may have noticed the bad weather lately. You and your dog are going to keep quiet about my presence, aren't you?"

It hadn't occurred to me to tattle. It had only occurred to me that I would have to go to battle with the bone shelf man. I realized I still had my pocketknife clenched in my hand. I slackened. "Of course not." Rhubarb sniffed the shelf, tottering.

"Your dog ain't always like that, is she?"

"No, sir. I'm here trying to find a cure. A sparrow led us here."

The bone shelf man nodded. "Always good to follow birds." He shuffled sideways, moving parallel to the shelves. "Dog needs a good bone. How about this one?" He gestured with his brows toward a giant, heavy bone labeled "mammoth" but from a cow. I picked it up. Rhubarb wagged her tail and whined.

"Don't give it to her yet. You got to carve a charm into it first." He nodded at my knife.

"What charm?"

"Your dog seems to need to calm herself. She needs some temperance. So, you carve a path up between some tall mountains, and then the sun rising above the mountains."

"That sounds complicated." I put the bone in my basket.

"Just put your intention into it."

"Thank you, sir." I stepped away.

"That's for your dog, now," said the bone shelf man. "Don't know what to do for you. Guess you need some more help."

I guessed so, though I still felt mighty.

The desert at night is colder than you or I imagine. I walked through the freezer section, past taquitos, pizzas, and ice cream sandwiches. I went through Women's Accessories. Workout equipment. Greeting cards. Scrapbook supplies. Toilet cleaner. Whine. "You can't have your bone yet, Rhubarbie. I haven't paid for it. And then I have to charm it."

I was looking at camping equipment when a Walmart employee approached me. She had somewhat successfully attempted to make her uniform of khakis and blue vest look flattering. Her nametag said, "Twilia," and she was wearing black nail polish.

"Can I help you find something?" asked Twilia, my angel-fairy, my witch-visiting sister in magic.

I told Twilia that I had been snapped, flooded, downed, and that I had gone to the witches so they could organize my emotions. I told Twilia that now I was straight, dry, and powerful, but that my dog

had been poisoned, and I wondered if I was too dried out.

Twilia looked at the heavy bone in my basket. "It seems like you need a little balance. Maybe you need a candle." She led me to the aisle of candles and potpourri, and we started smelling them. Sage-Melon. No. Lilac-Summer. No. Calming Beach. Red Wine Romance. Plumeria-Basil. No no no. Finally, I found one made of beeswax that smelled like yoga class.

Twilia smiled. "Just don't burn it all night."

"Why not? Will it mellow me out too much?"

"No. You just might burn your house down."

At home, I took down the "No, Thanks!" sign and replaced it with, "Not now, thanks, but maybe later." I plugged in my phone to charge but left it turned off. I did my best carving mountains and a rising sun into the bone and I did the same with my candle. I lit the candle. I put the bone on the kitchen floor. Rhubarb looked down at it from up on her hind legs and sniffed. I saw the bone tugging at her like a magnet; it twirled its lasso and roped her by the doggie shoulders. The candle burned and the bone stayed on the floor, and finally Rhubarb dropped to all fours, took the bone in her mouth, and trotted with it under the kitchen table to happily gnaw.

Once there was a coyote whose mother named her Mermaid. Once there was a coyote whose mother named him Gryphon. Once there was an orphaned coyote taken in by an animal sanctuary, and the humans named her Fairy Princess.

After years of drought, rain comes to the desert, and when the rains move on there is a super bloom. Blue bonnets, prickly pear, forget-me-nots, and pink buckeye. Carnation, sweet pea, you're doing great.

KURT LUCHS

MERELY BEING WALLACE STEVENS

The first time I read "Of Mere Being" by Wallace Stevens, I knew I had to memorize it. I could not proceed without this poem as part of my permanent mental furniture. No one but Stevens could have written it. In fact it's a tiny distillation of his lifelong mannerisms and obsessions into one concentrated dose, at twelve lines even shorter and more potent than a sonnet.

The exact date of composition is unknown, but most likely sometime in 1955, the last year of his life. One is therefore tempted, somewhat irrationally yet irresistibly, to view it as a summary or closing argument. Apparently Holly Stevens felt that way. When she edited a volume of her father's selected poetry in 1971, she titled it after the first line of this poem, *The Palm at the End of the Mind,* and gave it pride of place as the final poem in the book.

The title of the poem could serve as easily for a book of metaphysics or an essay by Francis Bacon, which is typical Wallace Stevens. He puts his philosophical preoccupations front and center. When originally published in *Opus Posthumous* in 1957, the last word of the first three-line stanza was "distance." Holly Stevens changed it back to the word used in the typescript draft, "décor." And that is a better word, such a Wallace Stevens word! Of course at the end of his mind there would still be something describable as a décor, and of course it would be bronze. Could this be the "bric-a-brac" that Robert Frost supposedly accused him of writing about?

The second stanza introduces the key image: "A gold-feathered bird / Sings in the palm, without human meaning, / Without human feeling, a foreign song." The movement from bronze to gold

subtly suggests being ushered into the presence of majesty. There the mind stops in its tracks, transfixed. What lies at the end of the mind, beyond the last thought, is a vision all the more compelling because it simply bypasses the intellect, making itself known only to direct apprehension. Suddenly the "mere being" of the title takes on new weight. Stevens plays on both of the main meanings of "mere," as in "smallest or slightest," and also "pure." In the former sense, ordinary, unexpanded consciousness (a "reducing valve," as Aldous Huxley called it) presents some everyday sensory data to us and reason steps in to analyze and interpret. In the latter sense, though, "mere being," pure being, cannot be interpreted by reason.

Thus the powerful realization that opens stanza three: "You know then that it is not the reason / That makes us happy or unhappy." The first two stanzas consist of a single sentence flowing smoothly like a film. The final two stanzas consist of six sentences, more like a quick succession of still photographs. The last line of stanza three contains two uncharacteristically concise sentences of three words each: "The bird sings. Its feathers shine." We can almost picture the poet's mouth agape with wonder. He's already told us the bird is singing. The reiteration has a bit of a hypnotic effect, or hints that the poet himself is under some kind of spell, perhaps his own.

The fourth and final stanza builds on everything that has come before. In a way it recapitulates the structure of the entire poem. It's a fractal, self-similar to the whole. First we notice the palm, which "stands on the edge of space." What space? Where? Let's leave those questions for the moment. In the second line we perceive something in the palm, but not yet the bird: "The wind moves slowly in the branches." Note that Stevens doesn't focus on the movement of the branches, but rather on what is making them move. He intuits the invisible by means of the visible. Because of this, and because wind is frequently used in religious literature as a metaphor for the spirit, this line is often taken to refer to a movement of the spirit. I believe this reading is correct.

The last line of the poem takes us by surprise, because up until that point Stevens doesn't employ a lot of the usual poetic devices. It's all imagery and plain talk. Only in this line does he overtly use alliteration and internal rhyme: "The bird's fire-fangled feathers dangle down." Obviously "fire-fangled" is the centerpiece of this line. There are more than 20,000 words in the English language. Like Shakespeare, however, Stevens did not find that to be quite enough for his purposes, so he invented one. The neologism "fire-fangled" conveys the meaning of "decked out," especially in a foppish manner, as well as the more archaic root meaning of "a silly or fantastic contrivance" (see Merriam-Webster). With this melodious line the speech of the poem becomes a song of praise and awe.

Naturally, Stevens being Stevens, and poetry being poetry, there are layers in this thing. The poem implies many questions, giving no answers but itself. Can we ever perceive reality directly? And if we could, what difference would that make in our understanding of it? If we are forever trapped in our own heads, is that internal universe any smaller or less mysterious or complex than the one around us? What if any is the relation between the two?

Like other Stevens poems-about-poetry, "Of Mere Being" both explores and enacts these unspoken yet very present questions. Whether space (external or internal) can have an edge, and whether anything lies beyond that, the poet encompasses all of it, planting a palm with a dazzling unknown bird in its branches to mark the occasion. He transmutes reason's wandering and wondering into primal wonder.

Kurt Luchs

Of "Of Mere Being"

Near the end, the poet sings of a palm
and a mysterious bird made of fire,
both just beyond the reach of his rational mind,

a mind that deals as readily with the duties
of an insurance executive as with
the astonishment of being Wallace Stevens.

Is the strange image of his own making
or is it a final gift from the universe
to its most ardent and articulate admirer?

Either way, he is transfixed with awe, we feel it
in the shortening sentences and the pure wonderment
of the music that emerges only in the last, lovely, unlikely line.

CHARLES HOLDEFER

Jeannie

Tim looked at his phone in the coffee shop and saw his own face. He didn't recall setting the camera for a selfie. He touched the control button to move on. Nothing happened. The face frowned. "Stop that!" it said.

Tim froze, staring at himself.

"Let me out."

Tim tilted his phone. "What the hell?"

"Let me out!"

"How do they do that?" Tim asked. "Does the app record me and somehow dub my words on top of the image?"

"You're not paying attention."

"It looks so real." Tim noticed his uneven collar and the circles under his eyes. He hadn't slept well last night, groping for his phone several times before dawn to check for a text message that didn't come. Now he straightened his collar. "OK, I'm going to move on. I've got stuff to do."

He put down his phone.

At nearby tables, people conversed or sat alone with their devices, sometimes smiling and reaching out to caress a screen. No one observed him.

After several sips of coffee, he was bored and picked up his phone again.

"Well?" his face said. "Thought you had stuff to do."

"I do. I want to call Jeannie. I need to check some information."

"Information? You mean like NASA data about ocean temperatures? A recipe for ceviche? Or maybe a video of cats with little boxing gloves on their paws?"

"That's nobody's business."

He tapped at his phone and then pressed firmly but nothing changed. He swiped repeatedly. His face grimaced but didn't go away.

"I can't . . ." Tim massaged an icon. "I can't even get emergency service. Enough, OK? This isn't funny anymore."

His face squinted at him. "*This* is the emergency."

The barista arranged a tray of muffins. A steamer hissed. Tim fiddled with a stir stick, pondering. In his disgust he'd turned off his phone and placed it across from him on the table as if it belonged to someone else. An invisible friend.

Right now, what he truly desired was to hear from Jeannie. Was she still asleep? He didn't give a damn about stupid cat videos or those other things. He'd anticipated a relaxing Saturday morning at the coffee shop, plotting his next move. Instead he was blocked.

"I'm outta here."

He stood up and slipped the phone in his pocket and left the coffee shop.

"'Whence knowest thou thy misery?'"
Jeannie had popped this question last week as they lay in bed and watched clouds move across her skylight. It was the fourth or fifth time he'd slept over. Cars hummed in the street below, and from the stairwell outside her door came occasional thumps as neighbors went to work. It was very cozy and Tim didn't want to move. She curled closer, adding, "The catechism tells us: '*Out of the law of God.*'"

"What are you talking about?"

With Jeannie there were always surprises. She had a grouchy cat named Lou who climbed surreptitiously onto shelves and when you least expected it, he would shoot out his paw and bat you on the head. Startled the bejeezus out of you. Or when Tim had texted "♥U!" for the first time, Jeannie had responded with some sexually explicit emojis that he hadn't known existed. This swiftly brought their relationship to another stage. And now, in bed under the clouds, Jeannie told him about her childhood.

She was a pastor's daughter and had grown up attending church three times a week. She knew the Heidelberg Catechism by heart. She had considered going into the ministry herself.

"You? Seriously?"

"Is that so surprising?"

Tim pictured her at work, poised in her blue suit, clicking through her PowerPoint. He was in logistics and Jeannie was a developer in human resources. The credo in Tim's department was *Right on time, every time!* Jeannie's brief included multiple project synchronicity and diversification. It was decidedly bigger picture.

"The only comfort is that you are not your own." She ran her palm across Tim's bare chest, adding, "*'Canst thou keep all these things perfectly?'*"

"Well, a guy can try."

"The catechism tells us: *'In no wise; for I am prone by nature to hate God and my neighbor.'*"

"Geez. That's pretty hardcore."

She kissed his ear and slid out of bed. "Sweetie, I'm not the one who said it." She went to the kitchen and put on the coffee machine. "Cereal OK?" she called. "Afraid I'm out of milk."

"That's fine."

Tim got dressed, and Jeannie tied on a kimono, blue with flaming orange tiger lilies. She clutched her cup with both hands, looking down into it.

"You believe all that?" he asked.

"I used to. It's how I was brought up, with redemption as the goal. That's the point. It's not as harsh as it sounds. There's something beautiful, actually. Putting everything in order, accepting a greater love."

Lou padded into the kitchen. He looked up with buggy eyes and let out a screaky meow. She pulled down a box of cat food.

"But then I couldn't muster it anymore," she said, shaking out nuggets. "It's a matter of faith, right? You have to believe it, not just say it. You shouldn't fake what you don't have."

Hearing her speak this way, Tim felt as if she'd invited him into new territory. It was like the first time they'd seen each other naked only more personal, like sharing a password.

Lou sniffed at the dry contents of his bowl.

"You want gravy, don't you?" she said.

Tim observed the parked cars and the sun on the sidewalk. I'm not going crazy, he told himself, touching the phone in his pocket. The world still looks the same. What would Jeannie think when he told her?

He spied a pay phone. Wow, what luck—these were hard to find nowadays. But when he drew nearer, he saw that it had been vandalized. A minute later he reached again to his pocket. He wanted to hear her voice. Maybe the settings in the phone's silicon brain had realigned their electronic synapses or whatever those little thingies were.

"So what's it gonna be?" his face told him.

"What do you mean?"

"*Think.* You paying attention?"

"Get out of my face!"

He stuffed the phone in his pocket and continued walking to Attucks Square where he sat on a bench. He stewed for several minutes until gradually his surroundings reset his thoughts. It was a fine day, no doubt about it, better out here than in the coffee shop. The air was sweet. A pair of sparrows hopped on the green with sudden, popcorn-like movements.

He'd left Jeannie a voicemail last night, suggesting that they meet for lunch at Kothu Kothu. It was a designer bistro whose interior featured live bamboo and a fountain. A plan had been taking shape in his mind, a plan that Tim rehearsed and petted. He saw himself and Jeannie at a table with starched linen and crystal, beside the fountain and its pool where koi carp lurked and waited, their large lips opening, closing. Tim ordered wine, which arrived in an icy bucket. The cork popped, the server poured. The koi mouthed a silent chorus of approval. And when Jeannie looked up with shining eyes and said *My, this is nice*, Tim would lean forward and announce: "I think we should move in together."

That was the plan. It was bold, a person could say he was rushing things. (How long had they been seeing each other? Two months and two days, precisely.) But he sensed that Jeannie wasn't afraid to be bold. It was time to embrace the future! They could set up house in one of those new duplexes by the river, on a street with a front yard, a tree, birds. Lou would like that.

Tim spent a quiet half-hour on the bench, alone with his thoughts. It was an unplanned diversion, like surfing on the inside.

He considered how his upbringing had been different from Jeannie's. His parents weren't anti-religious, exactly, but they'd been too frazzled to take their children to church. Fervor and catechismal rigor didn't register. His mother was a night nurse and on Sundays refused to leave her pajamas, while Tim's father, a junior high geography teacher who would roust his children on school days ("Up and at 'em! Time to milk the chickens!"), on weekends left them alone and retired to a shed in the back yard where he pretended to tinker while he drank.

As a teenager Tim had spent many Sundays at Doobie's Diner, where he bussed tables and learned other lessons. Once, a blizzard had blanketed the city, brought everything to a halt. The manager got stranded somewhere, leaving the young staff in charge.

It was like a holiday! They cranked up the music and joked cheekily with the few customers who straggled in; they played hockey in the kitchen with brooms and a bar of soap while the fry cook put up his feet and rolled a joint. Toward the end of his shift, a waitress named Loretta grabbed Tim by the back of his belt, turned him around and kissed him on the mouth.

Loretta Rinaldi. His first real romance, and the Sunday snowstorm had started it. Loretta was short and round and smart and had scored highly on tests and was applying to fancy private schools in hope of a scholarship and sometimes she corrected the speech of other employees, which didn't win her any friends, but Tim didn't mind, most of the time. Loretta was exotic. She cut her bangs in a severe straight line across her forehead and favored scarves that she referred to as *foulards*.

"Shall we then?" she said, nodding toward her coat, reminding Tim to help her put it on.

One day at the diner, a roly-poly lady with red cheeks sat at the counter eating pancakes and Loretta hovered over her with a pot of coffee and seemed very nervous. Tim wiped down a nearby table. As he moved away with a tray of dirty dishes, he joked with Loretta, "Your fan club is waiting for you in the kitchen."

"Is this Tim?" the pancake lady piped.

He stopped. "Hello."

"Loretta said you was a nice fella." She grinned at him, a dab of syrup on her chin. Loretta blinked and said nothing and in a flash he understood that this was Loretta's mother.

"Well," he replied, "Loretta is as fine as they come."

"Oh, she's a sweetie, she sure is." Mrs. Rinaldi stuffed a huge forkful of pancakes in her mouth, her eyes bright. Tim sensed that Loretta wanted him to go away, right now. He excused himself and returned to the kitchen.

Loretta didn't speak to him about the conversation with her mother, but in those days, after closing hours at Doobie's, she invited him to a walk-in storage closet where he sat on a chair and unzipped his pants and she stepped out of her panties and hiked up her skirt and straddled him. His hands clutched and roved, and Tim told himself: yes, now I'm entering the adult world.

But no. No. As he sat on a bench in Attucks Square, he could see that those rendezvous in the storage closet were just one of those teenage things, while the adult world resided in the unfinished conversation with Loretta's mother, which Loretta pretended had never happened. He'd gone along with the charade, because if he brought up the subject he knew it would embarrass her and she might put an end to their meetings in the storage closet. That had been his worry, when he was a kid.

Tim rubbed the side of his face, feeling a stab of tenderness for Loretta. He should've talked to her, made it clear that she had nothing to fear.

What is Jeannie afraid of? he wondered.

Tim got up and exited the square, passing dog walkers and food trucks. A kid thundered by on a skateboard. Without thinking, Tim took out his phone—a reflex, like scratching an itch—but he saw his face and instantly recalled his situation. "Oh God. It's still you."

"What do you want?"

"I want to use my damn phone!"

"Is that your only wish? Come on, dude. You're on a roll."

Tim swiped the screen but his face did not yield. He slapped the phone back in his pocket.

On the street he passed a pet boutique, a yoga studio, a closed bookstore. Rounding a corner, it occurred to him that he was only a five minutes from Jeannie's place. Roaming had taken him this far. Well, hell. He could arrive at her apartment—right on time!—and update her directly. A personal invitation would be better.

"Ring ring," he'd say.

"Hey!" She would smile. "What brings you here?"

"We got a beautiful emergency."

Tim turned onto Baywater Boulevard, and soon he reached Jeannie's building. He knew the four-digit code and let himself into the lobby, then climbed the stairs to the third floor.

He knocked on the door.

A man with a chipped front tooth answered. "Yes?"

Tim took one step backward—for a confused moment he thought that he'd knocked on the wrong door. But no. This was Jeannie's place, all right. The man wore gold wire-rimmed glasses and a tiger-lily kimono. "Who are you?" Tim asked.

"Who are you?" the man replied.

"Is Jeannie here?"

"No, she's out."

"Who *are* you?"

Footsteps sounded on the stairs and he turned to see Jeannie holding a yellow paper bag, which he recognized as coming from Badou Bakery, the best place in the neighborhood for fresh croissants.

"What are you doing here?" Jeannie asked.

"Didn't you get my message?"

"Yes, but . . . listen, Tim, I'm not available. I would've let you know if I was. We can talk about it another time, if you like. But you shouldn't just show up like this."

"I wouldn't have, but my phone isn't working."

"Whatever. Could you let me pass, please? This is not a good time."

At first Tim didn't move but she pressed forward, so he stepped back. There was a determination in her eyes that he hadn't noticed before. Jeannie entered the apartment, announcing, "Don't let Lou slip out." The man closed the door. Tim heard a murmur of voices on the other side, but he couldn't make out what they were saying.

Before leaving the building, Tim stopped and sat on the stairs. He spent several minutes there, rubbing his knees, breathing hard, trying to collect his composure. A boy with a basketball under his arm ran up the stairwell and then slowed down, staring as he passed, but Tim ignored him.

Later, back on Baywater Boulevard, he pulled out his phone. He wanted to talk to someone. A familiar face. But when he turned on the phone, it wasn't there.

The streets stretched before him, vast and bright.

JOHN PATRICK HIGGINS

CAFÉS OF DESIRE

"Is anyone sitting there?"

There was nobody sitting there. I confirmed this with haste that was just the right side of seemly. My body language changed. I pushed back into my seat and parted my legs. I was a chair asking her to sit on me. She didn't.

She quickly monopolised the table. I had a cup and saucer, spoon, an uneaten Italian biscuit, a notebook, a pen and a well-thumbed copy of Italo Calvino's *Mr Palomar*. These things were as nothing before the icebreaker of her handbag: the cup in its saucer chattered like teeth and the dog-eared book edged over the precipice. Her bag was large and black with pale cracks in the leather at each corner, fine as spiderwebs. There was something embossed on the side of the bag, or something had been pressed into its flesh. If it had once been legible, it was no longer the case: it was a scar now, pitted, semi-circular and with the gloss of skin mended over bone. The bag continued its voyage over the table, a black ship in full sail.

"Sorry," she said, diving into it and retrieving a pair of glasses, which she put on. The lenses were scratched and smudged with fingerprints, and I could hardly see her eyes through the scuffed refraction of the Café's strip-lighting. She whisked the bag off the table and onto her chair, rolling the coat from her shoulders and draping it over the chair-back. As she moved towards the counter, she half turned toward me: "Sorry. You don't mind, do you? The bag?"

"Of course," I said, meaning "Of course not." I looked at her, coolly. She was slim and tall, with dark curling hair. She leaned into the curving counter as she talked to the barista, her hips resting on the swell of the glass display case. Her nose, with the glasses resting on it, was long and sharp. I returned to my notebook, but my thoughts were distracted, my gaze inevitably drawn back to her animated discussion over the artisan sausage rolls.

I looked at what I had written. I had come to this café to steal. I was writing a novel about an isolated little man and I was here for verisimilitude: the conversations of old ladies and young mums, that sort of thing. Life experiences our hero would never know; happy people knitted into the community in easily defined roles: the salt of the earth next to my stultifying clod. But it wasn't working. Cafés were not the melting pots they used to be, at least this one wasn't. It was too upmarket. There was no grist. All human life was elsewhere—this was a middle-class verisimilitude I could fake in my sleep.

This part of town used to be dark with post-industrial grime. It was damp and clay grey and smelled of petrol and hard baked dust and lined your nostrils with black grit. Now it looked like every other part of town, any town. Though the coffee had improved.

I looked back at the counter and the girl appeared to be in the middle of an animated conversation with the server. It was familiar, as though they were old friends, though I had never seen her here before. Maybe she had that gift: she could just walk into a room and befriend it.

I picked up the copy of *Mr Palomar* and then looked again at my own inadequate scrawl. Calvino's prose was crisp and precise. The sentences were seamlessly dovetailed, even in translation. His writing was like a game of Jenga, sentences piled on top of one another, the process agonisingly teased out: the deliberate, detailed precision masking the writer's swagger, his poise. This was Calvino at the height of his powers, exulting in his own strength.

I had written this sentence: "Robinson pushed his hand into the belly of the sofa and met something warm and solid, something hairy and lively with jagged little teeth." I striped the page with a fat, black line and looked over to see the girl, but there was no sign of her. I looked at the bag. It was still there, the coat too. *Must have gone to the loo*, I thought.

I returned to the page, staring blankly at Robinson. I had no idea what to do with Robinson. I had forgotten who Robinson was. What sort of a name was Robinson anyway? No one was called Robinson: it was a barley water, a racist jam, a desert island dweller with a stirring theme tune. I had never met anyone called Robinson. It was an ersatz name: no one was called Robinson.

I ran another line through Robinson. It was a stupid, boring name and it was ruining my novel. How could someone called Robinson kill a vampire? Oh yeah, there are vampires in my novel. To kill a vampire, you must be Dutch, you have to be a "Van" something. But Van what? Helsing? Killsing? Horne? Gogh? Dyke? Dyke-Parks? The Man?

Forget the Van. It's been done to death.

How about Kincaid? Or Kindale? Carden? Clunes? Could a Clunes ever be a satisfactory protagonist in anything? Wishart? Bellamy? Benfield? Newman, Neumann, Garett, Parrott, Peters, Lee, Bassett, Bowley, Moncrieff, Hart, Atkins, Watkins, Pipkins. Smurfett, Parfitt, Rossi, Ball? Svenonius? Suzuki? Svenonius-Suzuki? Potter, Thatcher, Smith, Wainwright?

I was tentatively scratching in the name "Wainwright" when there was movement at the opposite side of the table. The girl was back.

"Thanks for looking after it for me," she said. "No problem," I said, looking up.

It was not the girl. It was certainly a girl, but it was not the girl, not the same girl.

"Sorry I was so long," she said. "No problem," I said, staring at her. She looked similar. Same build, same style of clothing. The hair was close. But they were not the same. If you'd seen her in passing you might have mistaken her for the same girl. But not me: I had looked properly, I had taken my time, and this was a completely different person. She reached for the handbag.

"What do you think you're doing?"

"What do you mean?"

"I'm watching that bag for someone."

"Yes. But I'm back," she said.

"Nice try," I said, coolly.

"It's my bag. You saw me put it here."

"No. I saw someone put that bag there and when she returns, I'll gladly give it back to her."

"It was me."

"C'mon!" There was an implied "love" at the end of the "c'mon", but I didn't say it in case it sounded sexist and patronising, even though I was in the right. "You haven't even tried: you're not dressed the same, your hair is wrong and, I hate to say it, but you're not as pretty. Sorry."

"I'm taking my fucking bag."

"No, you're not."

"Is there a problem?" said a passing barista, who may have been under the impression he was a policeman.

"I'm sorry?" I said, failing to recognise his authority, at least until he put the mop down. He directed the same question specifically to the girl.

"I asked this idiot to watch my bag and now he's saying it isn't mine."

"Well, it isn't."

"Oh, for fuck's sake!"

She swept up the bag and coat in a single movement and pushed into the street outside. I scrabbled to my feet, but the server blocked me.

"What are you doing? She's getting away."

"Leave it, sir," said the youth. The sir was a slight.

"You're abetting a crime," I said. We did a little dance, him jogging to one side in anticipation of me moving in that direction, and then moving in the other direction just as I had chosen to go that way. His shimmying would have been a boon to the Soul Train Line.

I scooped up my possessions, slipping the notebook, paperback and pens into the pockets of my raincoat.

"I have to go," I said. "I do not want to be here when the owner gets back." I punched my arms through the sleeves of my coat and limped toward the door as, in all the excitement, I hadn't noticed my foot had gone to sleep.

"I had a duty of care," I announced to the freshly interested café audience. They may have been middle-class, but they had the prurient appetite for spectacle of a nation raised on Jerry Springer. They were hoping for violence and confrontation and I was hoping to cheat them of it, though I would have welcomed the lie-detector test.

I went outside. The street was oblivious: men in baseball caps trundled over the uneven paving on mobility scooters. Pigeons stabbed at discarded chip packets. On the other side of the street a youth with an arm in plaster noisily failed to make another jump on a skateboard. There was no sign of the girl in the stolen coat with the stolen bag. I tried for a moment to put myself in her shoes, to try and imagine where a girl who had just successfully committed daylight robbery would go next. But almost as quickly as I started, I gave up. Because how could I possibly know?

Steven Breyak

Two Poems

Stepping from the Cabin

Subway to the airport. Osaka to Pittsburgh. Rent-a-car
nightmarc. Pittsburgh to Frazer Township. Predawn. 13-hour
jet lag like amphetamines clicked me on hours ago.
Time passed listening to the wood beams and tin roof creak,
 playing at what creature's traversing the woods just outside,
studying the nuances of sleep between my wife
and baby boy. At the first hint of light I make coffee
and head for the porch to watch the sunrise.

Stepping through the door a jolt shakes me. A spider
hangs before my nose. I had forgotten how prevalent
spiders are here. How I used to admire webs
pregnant with morning dew. In Osaka there is no dew,
and I only see spiderwebs occasionally packed thick
along bridge ledges. Country spider, city spider.
My wife would have me kill this one, but she's asleep
so I reach high and catch the thread on my finger.

A jolt again when the spider makes a quick climb
for my hand. I shake the silk away like it's burning,
search for a bite I'm certain I feel, but there's nothing.
I look back and she, the spider, still hangs there. What of what
happened happened? This time I catch the thread.
This time she doesn't move. Maybe she feels
her line arcing and gives way to the breeze I make.
I leave her dangling from the porch where I see other webs

 nested in the corners. A good place, I think. Her meals
 keeping pests from me and future guests. I feel pretty good
 about myself, like I did this spider right. Then I begin
 to think about whatever it was that moved me
 from my birthplace not far from this cabin to Asia,

to a life better than any I could have dreamed up here:
my wife, our son, a life that affords me this trip
home, time to sit and think up strange thoughts like this.

What finger from the sky moved my mind to fly out there?
Or here, on this page trying to shape the everyday
into something profound, to think someone would ever
care to see through me? I'd like to say to what-if-any hand
responsible, "Thank you" and "I'm terrified wondering where
your will ends and mine begins." I put
the pencil down. The sunrise long past, I look
for the spider and her work, but she's gone.

January 22nd, 2020

A summer night three years ago
I met a date for pizza.

A week after we met, I flew to the US
for a month. When I came back
we went out for takoyaki.

I was careful with my heart then.
I think we both were. We had both
mismarried before and were having
another go at youth.

And now she's asleep in the other room
with our son in her arms.

How did something so fragile
left to its own fate
grow into so much of why
I do anything?

Every day brings a happiness
I'd never known before.

Joe Taylor

Survival of the Fittest

1.

There'd been rumors, of course, for well over a century, of you and your mutation. I myself had espied a suspicious trio twenty years before. But when six of our outlying scroll depositories were burned and the survivors fled into our Neander valley home, we knew. The Cro-Magnons were coming.

Now, listen. Despite plethoric theorizing about chaos, no one believes its reality. Ask your neighbor. Just so. We ourselves, however, sustained no doubt about chaos: within our shadowy existence it had struck. Its butterfly had rippled, its horse threw a shoe, its supernova exploded, its COVID-19 bloomed, its differential equation skewed—all by ramming an invasive mutation known as Cro-Magnon upon us, led by a howler named Chuck Darwin.

The sole comment I can offer on Chuck's nomenclature is that stranger coincidences have occurred along the sidereal flow of the Milky Way. Name one, you say? Not me. It's *you* who've inherited the earth, not we meek Neanderthals, despite what our man Jesus will proclaim. Oh yes, *our* man. Why else would you so handily taskforce to dispatch him not thirty-three slim years after his birth? *If thine neighbor turneth the other cheek, crack it a good one, too.* See? Stranger things. But remember: the persistence of DNA, despite mutations, certainly belongs in that astounding conspiracy of strange.

So. When a sole survivor from a seventh (we too believed in numerical omens—who cannot place hope thereon?) a seventh scroll depository raid, when this survivor stumbled into our central settlement, we organized a moonlight meeting atop the Holy Rocks. I should describe the Holy Rocks. Our women called them the Holy Gonads; our men called them the Grand Tetons. Both nicknames caught, since we formed quite the egalitarian society. In some grand past, those Holy Rocks must have stood as a tremendous, tan monadic boulder, but eroding action of a long-gone river—read long-gone as in Homo Neanderthalensis—finally severed one boulder in twain, a telling precursor of Hinduism's corrupting veil of Maya long before Hinduism had blinked its blind third eye.

Be as be may, in moon's glow we gathered at the Holy Rocks. Our thirteen clan leaders leaned over the dividing cleft to hawk thirteen goobers. Such constituted our commencement ritual—much resembling the pre-game festivities for your North American Super Bowl. Then, standing high on the western Holy Rock, that seventh survivor related the gory vision of your coming, the coming of the Cro-Magnon. Why do I insist on writing "you" when *you* envision yourselves as so modern, so new, so homogenized, so sapient, instead of so *mutated*? Why, as you say, ask why? Cast into whatever *Homo Sapienic* century you choose: blood spatters here, blood spatters there. Thus your own *Homo Sapienic* Chuck Darwin got it almost right: not the vegetarian, pacific gorilla; not the happy, brachiating ape; but the gnashing, gorging Cro-Magnon served as your forebear. Only the brows have changed—certainly not to protect the innocent, but to disguise the guilty.

Back to that survivor: Declaiming from the western Holy Rock, he white-eyed toward coming night, "Skull pans split, to cradle the moon! Blood congealed, to paint midnight!" He paused for dramatics, being as he'd already crowed his tale a dozen times in the six-day interval since arriving. His pause effected a pleurisy: we wheezed, we shuffled, we studied our toes. "Panic! Everywhere!" he yelped. "**Panic, panic! Where, where!**" echoed from a nearby mountain's sheer granite walls. Adopting an ingénue mask, he continued chanting his diabolic litany: "Humerus, scapula, and tibia: snapped. Carpals, tarpals and metatarpals: crushed. Femurs, vertebrae, and skulls: scattered. Amid such carnage, I tripped over a ripped scroll on the ground and warbled, 'Feets, do your stuff!'"

Oh yes, we possessed refined language that could shift from tragic to comic faster than an udder's seepage—much faster and efficienter than any of your ridiculous Indo-European or Sino-Tibetan tongues, if you care to know. How about a word for "listless-love"? Do you possess one? Or what of the softness insinuating itself after a moon-cycle of meditative leisure? *Charmin* is as close as your languages will approach.

After this seventh survivor spoke, our thirteen clan leaders bled from wombs or emitted milk from vestigial nipples, each according to sex. Swirling the resultant liquids in an oaken bowl foretold—yes!—chaos and doom. In a fit of self-preservation one named Samuel took the speaker's position. From those Holy Rocks Samuel suggested setting up a thousand chess sets around our mountain perimeter, our vale of tears, the Neander valley. He further suggested we use these sets to challenge your forebears. Ah, just imagine:

"Whoa up there, Chuck! Yeah, you, big fella! Relinquish that bloodied club and sit down to a real man's game. Look! Look! See! See! Lo, I also have a flask of wine, and some pleasantly green olive branches!"

"Game? He'll think you mean Football or Drop-the-napalm-on-the-peasants!" our resident cynic shouted.

Though this acidic gentleman was booed down, I must note that no one seconded setting up those pacific chessboards, so the idea never came to Parliamentary vote. Instead, someone suggested we place sentinels to recite poetry to soothe the encroaching savages. A second supporter forwarded Kilman's "Tree" as most able to soothe beasts. *I*

think that we/ Will never see/ A poem as lovely/ As a tree. But dissenters worried that Kilman's very name might provoke violence, not peace.

As if inspired, a fellow named Matt clambered up the Holy Rocks to shout, "Sticks and stones!" We pictured a game, say "Counting Coup" like your North American Plains Indians would develop. But Matt meant his suggestion as—horror!—a brace of weapons. Realizing this, we unanimously—well almost unanimously, for one genetic toss-back started to snort a second to Matt's suggestion—overrode Matt's proposal. But on hearing pacifist inhalations sucking leaves and dislodging small vines from the Holy Rocks, that toss-back ducked. Following those inhalations, gaseous exhalations burbled through our Düssel stream as it flowed toward the Rhine, rendering it akin to bicarbonate of sulfur water, or perhaps one of your root beer soft drinks. In short, both Matt and the gentlemanly genetic toss-back had come very, very close to being ostracized from our peace-loving Homo Neanderthalensis clan.

"A utilitarian response. That's what we need," a chap named White Bread then suggested, taking his stance atop the Holy Rocks.

I'm going to pause and tell you how White Bread got his name, but let me preface an adjunctive scribble: Skim any modern health guide at Barnes and Noble and you'll learn that the darker the bread, the more opulent its vitamin-, mineral-, and protein-content. Conversely, the paler the loaf, the scantier. My point? White Bread—as will your European royalty and American Southern Belle (who, praise *People* magazine, will eventually render like so many vats of soured bacon)—I say that this White Bread lived even in our time as a throwback. Yes! For he abhorred not only texture, but any colorful tinting whatsoever in his loaves—to the extent of lopping off crust when making finger sandwiches for our bi-weekly scroll-rollings. Hence his name.

"A utilitarian response is what we need," he reiterated.

Hereto, White Bread and utilitarian would have been classified as oxymoronic, but if anything, we Neanderthals stand willing to listen:

"The meat-gnashers can't be stopped by reason, any more than by extravagant diversions." White Bread gave a glance to Samuel, still pouting over the chess sets. "And we Neanders," White Bread continued, "certainly aren't burdened with the crass digestive glands necessary to use force." White Bread glared about for Matt, who'd slunk under a Gloria Bush, the only plant red enough to cover his shame at suggesting violence. In the ensuing silence, our gentlemanly resident cynic stirred from a catnap: "Hey, how about a food fight?" But White Bread's heavy brows ignored that catcall to proclaim, "The good of the many overcomes the good of the one."

He paused.

We thought.

Any platitude always must be mulled over, must it not?

"We *are* the many, *and* we *are* the good," he continued, giving a bona fide White Bread sigh.

"Get on with matters!" I fear that this emitted from our ever-present cynic, who busily shook his ears to rattle mites. So now he was not only completely awake, but angered at having his one-liner about a food-fight ignored. His shout was met with serious nods: brows dented earth, pressing their ponderous bone matter downward. By the wayward way, did you know that the sinuses in our huge brows afforded extra passages for circulating brain fluid? Of course not, your physical anthropologists surmise our heavy brows served only as prototypical football helmets. *Pro-ject-shun*—our man Freud, oh how he'll try his hardest to enlighten you about *that* itty-bitty concept.

"I will get on with matters," White Bread huffed. As he exhaled, refined flour sifted from his lungs.

"Our women . . . must give themselves to the beasts."

Even our cynic was appalled. Overhead, a star gave blink. It was, as you might guess, Venus. Of course we knew that Venus wasn't a star, though I must assert that *your* Cro-Magnon ancestors (*Ugh-ugh, speaken sie la Indo-europeenish?*) had no such discernment availing their paws/craws/jaws. And to twist the screw, didn't your own *Homo Sap* Ptolemy conjecture that the stars were little twinkle-lights shining through a restful Super Dome? Hurricane Katrina, anyone?

Two more asides, if you can bear them: Firstly, our man Immanuel Kant will someday preach that the highest form of virtue is to act for virtue itself, not for any deed's petty utilitarian result. Damn him to Hades for that mutant, Cro-Magnon mix! Who could imagine this thought emitting from a man who will mandate "The starry skies above, the moral law within" engraved upon his tombstone? Nonetheless, emit it he did. Secondly, our men Watson & Crick will start what your two commercial laboratories will finish: the mapping of the—ahem—*human* genome. And here—thanks so lovekindly for your patience with my ramble—*here* is how the two asides combine: Both virtue *and* deed are important.

Standing under the pale light of Venus, we grasped what White Bread was suggesting: Exterminate the brutes, yes. Not by clubs, spears, or arrows, but by love, by sacrificing our very selves. Hundreds of our peaceful folk fainted. An abominable thought, to mingle not only our bodies and fluids with the beast, but to mingle our very genes. Yes, the supreme virtue of self-sacrifice for racial preservation would require the deed of our own (wo)man-handling of chaos.

2.

At that moment, Chuck topped a mountain crest. Too stupid to weave a banner, he and his clan had uprooted saplings, as if playing bit roles in *MacBeth*—need I mention that Shakespeare was another of our men? "Peas and carrots! Peas and carrots!" Chuck and his crew shouted as they thrust the saplings in violent, cyclical motions. A cynic, if one had been present, would have thought, *Truly, the illiterate shall inherit the earth.*

"*Consummatum est!*" Someone yelled. Ah, so our gentlemanly cynic *was* present—he'd just paused to grab his breath. We looked to the mountain's crest. There was time enough to dab our women with perfume, comb their hair, and apply a hint of rouge from some lingering rose blossoms. As they sashayed, we men sat calmly behind chessboards or raised poetry books . . . for hope, it does ever so spring, ever so eternal, and who could tell what might turn Chuck aside?

Now a cynic's life is a wholesome one. No scroll, no chessboard, but a quiver of arrows, a bow, and two semi-brachiating arms lifted him up into a bo-bo tree. The bo-bo, extinct by your time but indigenous to Neander Valley, emitted exotic, fragrant blue-green nectar. Its branches, wide and dense, spread parallel to the ground in the same fashion as those of a live oak. We typically used the bo-bo for meditation or relaxed courtship rites. But a cynic knows no bounds, so up the tree I clambered, while the remaining males awaited their deaths below, stoically abiding in those "peace-making" poetic or chess-boardish poses I've described.

I suppose that something of an I-told-you-so urged me up that bo-bo. Twenty years before, after sighting that trio of Cro-Magnons grimly gutting a wolf even while it was dying, I'd urged that we migrate far from your wretched meat-eating Indo-European ancestors, for my single hour's exposure told me that accidental laughter or even a brief smile would literally crack their thin, jutting jaws. Believe me; no brain fluid flowed through those mandibles; they were much too brittle even for spittle.

There was another purpose for the bo-bo, other than meditation or lovemaking. This also urged my climb. In our funeral rites, each of-age family member would ascend a bo-bo to soliloquize the departed one. Purging was the intent, not communing with ghosts. In solitary chant we would re-cant the beloved's life, and we would soon hear, through auditory trance, our own future biography, as if some future grandson or –daughter were also chanting. Such a trance always improved individual lives. To my mind, this practice served as our civilization's cornerstone. *Bo thyself*, to mangle a future Greek's phrasing. And yes, of course, Socrates was one of ours. Don't you just know it? *Bo thyself.*

So I climbed and hid amid thick rubbery leaves. Chuck trotted his band down from the mountain with the expected Indo-European grunts, "Hut-hut, hold that line! Block that punt!" Poetry scrolls were kicked aside, chessboards scattered. How quickly, I realized on hearing the dull thud of clubs, can the smell of death fill the air. Each descending club lifted flecks of flesh and droplets of blood to create a low-hanging haze that clogged my lungs and oppressed my bones, much like an ominous storm system. For the melee's duration, our men and male children died in stoic silence, while Chuck and his carnal gang war-whooped like hyenas. Since no resistance was offered, the massacre was soon completed.

The Cro-Magnons turned toward our women. Now, our own lovemaking in the bo-bo was Edenic. Side-by-side, often in the glow of a full or gibbous moon, though sunrise or sunset would also suffice, we would lie. Side-by-side on a generously wide branch of a bo-bo, we would lie, roll, and inhale. Amidst a caress we might talk of a departed family member, remembering his or her smile or some humorous anecdote. In this meditative leisure would we procreate. Our unspoken practice: whatever celestial cycle incited the lovemaking would also end it. If the lovers began at moon's rising, they continued until its setting. From dawn until dusk, or dusk until dawn. There were even couples who would put by water and food enough to use the moon's full cycle for an episode of lovemaking, from full to waning.

Chuck and his Cro-Magnons held no such beliefs.

Like frogs they hopped. Like frogs they slimed.

Evening was my life-mate's name. What I now remember most about Evening in my approaching senility are her eyes, hazel and sanstsumi in nature. Pardon me. I've slipped into our expedient and loving tongue. "Sanstsumi" is a quality of eye/personality indicating a great, deep-moving freedom. Such was Evening, and such were her eyes.

How painful, then, to watch her frantic eyes directly beneath the bo-bo whereon I perched. She lay not side-by-side with the brute to make love, but endured his sweating, weighty compression of her sanstsumi. The missionary position, I understand you call it. More like the mission position. Thrusting, thrusting—until Evening's lovely eyes bulged in animal shock. Thrusting, thrusting. No words, only grunts and passed gasses. Thrusting, thrusting. In the bo-bo I started a low chant, from whence—other than the ethics of Immanuel Kant—I know not: "Not the deed, but the virtue. Not the deed, but the virtue. Not the deed, but . . ." Kant's maddening cant and the Cro-Magnon's thrusting, thrusting, echoed off the bo-bo until I could no longer hold back: I strung a Zen arrow and sent its flight true. Zen not Zeno, for my arrow had no trouble with halfway points mysteriously repeating unto infinity. Upon its impact the brute exploded sexually, his petit and grand mort coinciding. Who can ever end so fortunately, I rationalized. But I didn't need rationalization, for Evening had endured the deed. She had performed her ethical duty; she had mated with the simian Cro-

Magnon. But just where, we wondered, did virtue abide? In some starry constellation? I think not.

Climbing down, I feared that in my anger I'd mistakenly shafted the arrow into Evening too, for she lay inert. Not so. I peeled the brute's body off and we escaped to higher ground. Higher yet harsher. In that cold climate we soon learned exactly where virtue resided, for the deed had been consummated, and yes, Evening was carrying a Cro-Magnon half-breed in her womb. We—she!—had accomplished White Bread's prescribed goal.

3.

It is written in our prophetic scrolls that the Buddha, he born Siddhartha Gautama, will take seven steps after emerging from his mother's side. He will announce, "This is the last time I shall be born." Similarly, our Neanderthal newborns would always grin upon emerging from the womb, toss both hands in a welcoming mystic pose, and intone, *"Go gallá-pa-go!"* Which in your language roughly means, "Give praise for the everlasting onrush of time!" What, Evening and I wondered, would this new sub-species do?

We counted the months. Finally, Evening squatted over cushioning bo-bo leaves to give birth. The newborn cried; it squinted in ruddy Cro-Magnon hue; it squeezed its tiny paws in an egoistic grip. It gave no indication of Neander Valley's spiritual awareness, no joyous shout. The deed appeared to be a failure.

Not the deed, but the virtue, I reminded Evening and myself. *Not the deed, but the virtue.* Could Immanuel Kant be right? Could suffering and self-denial remain worthwhile, though patently a failure? Not only Evening but all of our women had willed good—wasn't that enough? *Not the deed, but the virtue.* I looked to the starry skies above but envisioned only the crushed males of our soon-to-be extinct species splayed at the massacre site. I envisioned our women made sex objects and slaves. Not the deed, but the virtue sent a sickening ring.

As a final symbol, a pellet of meconium dropped from the newborn's rear end. I pulled Evening away from the befouled bo-bo leaves. Evening's eyes did not reflect sanstsumi; they drizzled animal tears. We trod heavily from the newborn creature; but on our seventh step we heard— not our Neander Valley ritual of praise shouting out, to be sure, but a gurgling laugh. What!? We turned. We saw the newborn opening his left hand toward an owl in a nearby tree. That gurgle-laugh again.

I am a cynic, not a romantic. The owl wanted food, it was not delivering omens of wisdom; the infant's gesture was reflex unfolding, not an international plea for world peace. But that half-gurgle, half-laugh could mean only one thing: in Hegelian give-and-take (need I mention that Hegel was one of ours?) deed had rekindled virtue. Loss had forged love. The many had won, the fittest would survive, our Neander Valley line would live. How else, I ask you, could a simplistic Cro-Magnon/ Homo sapiens mix ever produce Jesus, Freud, Watson, the Buddha, Hegel . . . or Immanuel Kant? How? I'll tell you how: The starry skies above, *Go gallá-pa-go!* within.

Aaron Anstett

Report from the Apocalypstaycation

[from Quarterly Report]

The messages we expected failed to appear.

While we longed for a color to echo,
foreign powers weaponized the voluble gullible.

In sleep the phrase "lollygag sonnets" repeated.

I formally request a dispatch from the realm
of The Impossible Happenstance and world map
shimmering with the glint of sunlight
on bottles' lips in ditches.

*

May all particles and forms align
themselves in alphanumerish order.

Neighbors lightheadedly alert one another.

Thank you, Von Quaglio, who first added
mercaptan to scentless natural gas
and imbued it with a startling odor.

May all breathing beings inhale,
exhale, inhale, exhale over and over.

*

From one idea a musculature
emerges, strung with nervous
system and various purposes.

Hands began to grab branches.

Then defensive architecture benches
kept the unhoused from resting.

Among the stars, a shape
of tracery's glittering trickery.

*

Who believes the skin
an archive of scars?

The past and its structures
disappeared to dust
and ash and mist?

Eels wriggle great distances
from rivers, streams, and creeks
back to the Sargasso Sea, fins
expanding as they swim.

*

I'm calling the new book
Late-Stage Everything.

As aforementioned, I like best
exactish measurements, your
soupçon, your smidgen, your little bit.

Things that sound more fun
abstract than actual: fiasco, criminal mischief.

We're all equally susceptible to the universe's tactics.

Pack sufficient ammo and snacks
for the coming apocalypstacation.

We'll survive with gumption and serum
of mescaline and adrenaline.

*

Here on out let us close every document
 "The apocalypse barges in all
be-all end-all, bullying and bossing
atoms and orbits around."

The largest hummingbird on earth
in Bolivia is known as *burro q'enri*,
Spanish *burro* for its dull plumage.

I see the name written in a founding
document's frilly script. Imagine
the body less noun than verb,
event that ends. What is said

sotto voce, held gently
in the cupped palms of parentheses?

*

No responsible medical professional
attaches a prehensile tentacle

to a man's head to distract
from bald spot. But I want it

all and soon: Dead friends breathing
again, exact food for every hunger,

prosthetic arms but real fingers,
to have whatever kills me kill me

quick, lickety-split, swift
as current through water, as flick of wrist.

You Again

You were you but not you,
you know, like in dreams,
or the infinite repetitions
on which two mirrors
facing each other insist.
Pillows await lucky
and cement less-lucky heads.
Bodies auger all manner

of onslaught, respite, beds.
Like me I imagine you glad
regardless in whatever conditions—
sunlight, snowstorms—
happy to be there, feeling it
an honor just to be considered.

Until All the Otherwise We Wish

You may as well ask a taxidermied animal—
hide stretched on armature, eyes
polymer resin, posed in lifelike manner—
"What happened?" as demand the minuscule
particles of atoms, obstinately animate,
stand still. How do the gods respond
to hosannas and uvula-quivering hallelujahs?

Aspens trembling in a meadow are one
being's tendrils, ringed by cartoonishly
colossal rubble. Replacement molecules
and cells align in a body's particular
patterns, even tattoos of scripture and/or
chimera, impossible, mashup animal.

Ex Cathedra All the Live-Long Day

Enthroned, bath-robed in imagined
sanctum sanctorum, I steeple
my fingers and pronounce
stoic Latin maxims ineptly. Mostly
they exhort to brace ourselves
for the body's built-in obsolescence,
its time-release indignities.

Be glad at least once an isolated
drop of rain, all surface and interior,
magnified the full moon's flecked panache.

Let God or whatever iffyness
rush between hearts. *Abstruse*
should be the color and/or name of a flower
whose innards I inhabit, occupied
by prolonged, inconclusive thinking about a matter.

David Collard

On James Hadley Chase

Who, these days, reads *No Orchids for Miss Blandish* by James Hadley Chase? The author's first novel, it was written over the course of six weekends and originally published in Britain in 1939, when Chase was 33. Widespread condemnation of its explicit scenes of sex and violence did no harm at all to sales which soon exceeded half a million, although US publication in 1942 caused less of a sensation among readers familiar with the hard-boiled fictions of James L. Cain. It was surprisingly not banned at the time but became, and remains, a benchmark publication when it comes to the depiction of what we now call 'adult themes'.

James Hadley Chase (1906 – 1985) was born René Lodge Brabazon Raymond and after an unpromising start—he was employed as a door-to-door encyclopaedia salesman—had an astonishingly prolific career, publishing more than ninety novels of which fifty were made into films, more than thirty of them French movies. Thanks to Éditions Gallimard, who continue to publish Chase under their Série noire imprint, he is one of the few British writers to command a large following in France. In Le Monde's 100 Books of the Century *No Orchids for Miss Blandish* comes in at 89, immediately behind *The Catcher in the Rye*.[1]

On reading the first page you might be surprised to learn that the author was British. Here's how it opens:

> IT BEGAN on a summer afternoon in July, a month of intense heat, rainless skies and scorching, dust-laden winds.

At the junction of the Fort Scott and Nevada roads that cuts Highway 54, the trunk road from Pittsburgh to Kansas City, there stands a gas station and lunchroom bar: a shabby wooden structure with one gas pump, run by an elderly widower and his fat blonde daughter.

A dusty Lincoln pulled up by the lunchroom a few minutes after one o'clock. There were two men in the car: one of them was asleep.

The driver, Bailey, a short thickset man with a fleshy, brutal face, restless, uneasy black eyes and a thin white scar along the side of his jaw, got out of the car. His dusty, shabby suit was threadbare. His dirty shirt was frayed at the cuffs. He felt bad. He had been drinking heavily the previous night and the heat bothered him.

Writing in the October 1944 issue of Horizon magazine, George Orwell expressed both admiration and dismay at the astonishing success and popularity of the novel.[2] Of Chase's near-perfect American prose style, Orwell remarked that many English readers were partly Americanised not only in their language but also in their moral outlook, sharing the American tendency to tolerate crime and even to admire the perpetrators so long as they are successful.

This new tolerance was a change in public values that disturbed Orwell, who compared the huge popularity of Raffles the gentleman thief, a modest canon of 26 short stories and one novel by E.W. Hornung, (brother-in-law to Sir Arthur Conan Doyle), all published between 1899 and 1909. These fictions, Orwell observed, while not in the least offensive, shared with *No Orchids for Miss Blandish* a focus on the criminal rather than the agencies of law enforcement. They also shared a moral compass, or lack of one.

It's not so much the moral compass that interested Orwell, but what might be called the moral barometer—the very different auras surrounding the Raffles stories and *No Orchids for Miss Blandish*, and the extent to which the huge popularity of the latter reflected a change in public taste.

While Hornung's stories retain a period charm, are technically accomplished and undeniably entertaining, Orwell points out that their enduring appeal stems from the fact that the upper-middle class Raffles, while not quite an aristocrat, is certainly a gentleman and, as the product of a public school education who has gone off the rails, both a renegade and an outcast. Though seldom subject to reflection or remorse, he sometimes feels that he has disgraced 'the old school' (never specified; let's assume it's Orwell's alma mater Eton). He is therefore a cad (one who behaves badly) but not a bounder (one who behaves in an ungentlemanly way)—a distinction now lost to us. The point is that a toff as a burglar is a much more alluring prospect than, say, a greengrocer or plumber, who would be criminals merely.

He's an all-round sportsman with a particular flair for cricket, a game which, Orwell notes, embodies 'a well-marked trait in the English character, the tendency to value 'form' or 'style' more highly than success". Cricket is the traditional stronghold of 'fair play', that elusive and defining quality of the British and, by making Raffles both an accomplished amateur cricketer and a skilled amateur cracksman, Hofnung made clear the ethical difference between public persona and private practice, and the social gulf between the paid professional and the dedicated amateur.

Cricket at that time made a clear demarcation between 'gentlemen' and 'players'—another distinction now lost—and was one in which it was not unusual for the unremunerated gentlemen amateurs to excel over the paid professional players. The cult of the amateur, and the ruling class's aloof disdain for anything that smacks of diligence or earnestness, or of professionalism, for anything as dull as hard-won expertise, continues to afflict British society and politics to this day.[3]

While Raffles has no clear moral code, no religious beliefs, no political allegiances and no social consciousness, he does have explicit standards which his readers are expected to admire and invited to share. Urbane, witty and smart, he has,

among other skills, "the subtle power of making himself irresistible at will", at least according to his devoted accomplice Bunny (they are much more of a couple than Holmes and Watson). As a 'gentleman' he is high spirited, daring (reckless even), chivalrous, a loyal friend and stoutly patriotic. His crimes, though not victimless, are relatively and tolerably innocuous—the theft of jewellery from a wealthy house guest for instance. Robbing from the rich and pocketing the proceeds is halfway to being a modern day Robin Hood.

And it all boils down to snobbery, of course. Horning's readers like to know about goings-on in high society, a world from which they are excluded. Raffles is not from the top drawer so his social position, while lofty, is insecure; the 'gentleman burglar', like the homosexual, lives in constant fear of exposure and expulsion and is therefore obliged to act covertly. 'We were in Society but not of it' says Raffles to Bunny at one point, meaning that they are both bound by the standards of a society, in which 'the done thing' is understood, if seldom defined.

So much for standards. Now, warns Orwell, turning to *No Orchids for Miss Blandish*, for 'a header into the cesspool'. He starts by listing, with a kind of fastidious relish, the contents:

> eight full-dress murders, an unassessable number of casual killings and woundings, an exhumation (with a careful reminder of the stench), the flogging of Miss Blandish, the torture of another woman with red-hot cigarette-ends, a strip-tease act, a third-degree scene of unheard-of cruelty and much else of the same kind.

If this sounds more like a Quentin Tarantino scenario than a 1930s novel it barely scratches the surface. Here's what happens, with plenty of spoilers:

A gang of crooks led by a grifter called Riley plan to steal a valuable necklace belonging to a millionaire's daughter. This unambitious crime results in her abduction, and a murder, and the arrival on the scene of a competing mob led by one Ma Grisson and her psychotic son Slim. He decides to kidnap Miss Blandish from Riley's gang and claim the ransom from her wealthy father, who has enlisted Dave Fenner, a former journalist now a private detective, to rescue his daughter. To complicate matters she has fallen for Slim, in an early fictional depiction of what would in the 1970s be called Stockholm syndrome. When separated from her rapist lover she throws herself from a skyscraper.

The modern reader, both jaded and critically alert to all things 'problematic', may find it hard to imagine the impact, eighty years ago, of a passage such as the following:

> Slim, still grinning, held the knife-point just below Riley's navel and put his weight on the handle. The knife went in slowly as if it were going into butter. Riley drew his lips back. His mouth opened. There was a long hiss of expelled breath as he stood there. Tears sprang from his eyes. Slim stepped back, leaving the black hilt of the knife growing out of Riley like a horrible malformation. Riley began to give low, quavering cries. His knees were buckling but the cord held him up. His weight on the ropes pushed the knife handle up so that the blade slowly cut deeper inside him.
>
> Slim sat on the grass a few feet away and gave himself a cigarette. He pushed his hat over his eyes and squinted at Riley.
>
> 'Take your time, Pal, We ain't in a hurry.' He gave him a crooked smile as his fingers traced the sky. 'Ain't them clouds pretty?'

Orwell is at pains to point out that the novel is not in any sense negligible trash but 'a brilliant piece of writing, with hardly a wasted word or a jarring note anywhere'. What troubles him is the motive that drives the story: the pursuit of power or, as he had put it in his essay 'The Lion and the Unicorn' five years earlier, the power-worship that had infected the British intelligentsia but had not, until then, touched 'the common people'. Orwell's most unsettling claim is that 'the mental atmosphere of these books [i.e. pulp fictions of the Hadley Chase kind] is [. . .] the struggle for power and the triumph of the strong over the weak.' They are, he argues, essentially fascistic in tendency.

The modern reader will probably disagree with Orwell's claim that 'the scenes describing cruelty to women are 'comparatively perfunctory'—Miss Blandish is flogged with a rubber hose and repeatedly raped by her abductor—but harsher cruelties are indeed inflicted by men on other men, and described in far greater detail, such as the stomach-turning torture of a minor character called Eddie Schulz.[4]

Adventure stories offer readers a vicarious sense of agency. There are escapist freedoms to be found in a work of pulp fiction that are simply unavailable in daily life, especially during war time, when days and nights are a mixture of boredom and fear. In fiction we are as readers at most at one remove from the centre of things. In an air raid we are entirely passive and helpless.

No Orchids for Miss Blandish marks a turning-point in popular British fiction because of the author's equivocal attitude towards crime and the loss of any clear distinction between what is right and wrong. In Chase's novel there is in fact no straightforward 'right' at all, only varying degrees of wrong, and the conventions that had once circumscribed Raffles, that crime does not pay and that virtue must win out over vice, no longer apply. Any sharp distinction between right and wrong, and between legality and illegality, has either become blurred or simply disappeared. To be sure this was familiar terrain for American readers of pulp fiction, but this was something new in Britain.

Chase was also something new in British fiction: a popular writer devoted to 'realism', defined by Orwell as the doctrine that might is right. Orwell connects (but does not take the time to explore) the links between sadism, masochism, success-worship, power-worship, nationalism and totalitarianism, a subject he admits, tongue in cheek, is a 'delicate' one. What disturbs Orwell is that the escapism offered by Chase is not into an imaginary realm of adventure, but into one of cruelty and sexual perversion—of depravity.

Orwell claimed that several readers had told him that Chase's novel was 'pure Fascism', but pointed out that while this was unarguably the case, it was in no sense a political novel, having the same relation to fascism as Trollope's novels had to nineteenth-century capitalism. *No Orchids for Miss Blandish* is, he concludes, resonantly, 'a daydream appropriate to a totalitarian age'. 'People worship power in the form in which they are able to understand it' he writes, quotably, before concluding with an hilarious take down of Bernard Shaw—but you'll need to read the whole essay (available online) to find out why.[5]

[1] Raymond Queneau adapted the plot from *No Orchids for Miss Blandish* as the basis for his novel *On est toujours trop bon avec les femmes* (1947, translated into English as *We Always Treat Women too Well*).

[2] "The Ethics of the Detective Story from Raffles to Miss Blandish". *Horizon* Vol. 10 issue 58,. October 1944

[3] The cult of the amateur has afflicted Britain throughout history: Churchill's 'Keep Buggering On', the current government's disdain for experts, the discourse surrounding Brexit, the mismanagement of the Covid crisis, the block-headed cockbluster of Boris Johnson and his biddable kakistocracy and so on, and on.

[4] There's a foretaste of Orwell's celebrated 'vision of the future' in *Nineteen-Eighty-four* (which would be published in 1949) when he cites another Chase novel *He Won't Need It Now* (published, like *No Orchids for Miss Blandish*, in 1939) in which the hero 'is described as stamping on somebody's face, and then, having crushed the man's mouth in, grinding his heel round and round in it'. One can imagine Orwell squirrelling this horribly violent image away for future use. Indeed, he would use the image in his 1939 essay 'The Lion and the Unicorn': "The goose-step, for instance, is one of the most horrible sights in the world, far more terrifying than a dive-bomber. It is simply an affirmation of naked power; contained in it, quite consciously and intentionally, is the vision of a boot crashing down on a face."

[5] After the war *No Orchids for Miss Blandish* was successfully adapted for the stage and filmed (atrociously) in 1948. It may be the film version that sank the novel's reputation; it was, according to Leslie Halliwell, a 'hilariously awful gangster film [and] one of the worst films ever made'. The novel remained for a time, in those far-off years before the Lady Chatterley Trial and the beginning of sexual intercourse, a byword for literary depravity, especially among those who hadn't read it, until its position was taken by *Lolita* (first published in Paris in 1955). It was the sort of thing Tony Hancock would read on a wet Sunday afternoon, slouched on his sofa bedsit (and in fact it was the Hadley Chase-esque *Lady Don't Fall Backwards* by Darcy Sarto that the lad himself struggled with in *The Missing Page*).

REVIEW | Liam Bishop

Someone to Rely On

Siphonophore
Jaimie Batchan
Valley Press, Feb. 2021

It's not immediately apparent what the significance of siphonophore are to Batchan's novel, which opens in 1701. Carl Linnaeus—the 'father of modern taxonomy'—won't discover the Portugese Man o' War for another fifty-seven years (often mistaken for jellyfish, the 'Physia Physalis' are actually colonial animals, consisting of numerous single animals—or zooids—connected to one another, and otherwise known as siphonophore). Besides, a hefty crew of Scottish sailors have a lot worse to contend with. Landing on a narrow strip of land connecting North and South America (Darien, the Isthmus of Panama), the crew from the Kingdom of Scotland are hoping to utilise this strategic stronghold and establish New Caledonia. The voyage, however, hasn't gone to plan, and the marooned crew wonder about their fate.

Our narrator, 'fortune seeker, citizen of Darien and Protagonist', MacGregor, keeps the reader informed of events. As well as speaking out to the reader, MacGregor speaks out to the Council about the New Caledonians' dire conditions: with a flotilla of Spanish aggressors on the horizon, the crew need to establish defences. But even this is botched, and they eventually find themselves leaving Darien, apart from MacGregor. '[A]bandoned amidst the last crumbling connection to my own people,' he tells us, 'I began to commune with my Creator.' MacGregor isn't talking about or to a holy deity though, he's talking about the writer of the novel in which he's encased.

MacGregor recognises Robinson Crusoe is 'the entity with whom I share so much'. This is true, but how does he know Defoe's novel won't be published for 'another nineteen years'? It isn't entirely implausible—Daniel Defoe was a popular, if dissenting, journalist and pamphleteer at the time of the New Caledonian's voyage, so perhaps MacGregor might have had an inkling of Defoe's later creation. It's when MacGregor shows cognizance of his 'Creator's' 'divine processes' that we really begin to wonder what kind of entity MacGregor is. He watches his Creator use Wikipedia, make coffee, and visit his GP.

It's here we learn why MacGregor is so invested in his Creator's processes: his fate ultimately resides in his Creator's ability to finish the novel. Completion is going to be difficult. The Creator, we learn, suffers from a rare—and real—condition known as Prionic Fatal Insomnia. A frankly terrifying prospect for the sufferer, who experiences progressively worse insomnia and, eventually, death. MacGregor witnesses his Creator undergo 'sleep hygiene assessments', 'multiple sleep latency tests,' 'actigraphs', 'polygraphs', and other observations. All very diligent and clinical. The modern clinical world, however, really bristles up against MacGregor's:

> We brought a physician to Darien, but very little medicine was practised. Healthcare amounted to the allocation of bitter herbs, or horrifying ordeals of surgery when nature demanded a more radical solution. Prayer was our repeated prescription, but the modern world has moved on. My creator's appointments are coordinated through his GP. He's been swiftly processed by the machinery of the National Health Service. He wanders through corridors reading the signs: ENT, paediatrics, nephrology, tropical medicine; endless avenues of specialisation.

Batchan constructs his own isthmus here: he swiftly connects the typhoid-ridden world of New Caledonia with the modern healthcare system in that middle sentence, '[p]rayer was our repeated prescription, but the modern world has moved on.' The modern world is always moving on for MacGregor; it's the frequent appointments and 'endless avenues of specialisation' of the Creator which are at odds with MacGregor's world of 'radical solutions' and getting the job done in a hurry. Although we might ask of the Creator why they find it so difficult to finish what they started, MacGregor seems to ask, why don't we turn away from those who claim to have put us here in the first place, even when they don't treat us well? Indeed, MacGregor mentions Job on a couple of occasions, and it raises the question—whether it's God, our parents, our seemingly fictional creators—of why we bestow them with the power to do as they wish. MacGregor is holding his Creator to account.

There are a couple of questions, too, for Batchan, the real fictional creator of these worlds. As the novel veers toward more voice and abstraction, it seems almost neglectful to research this historical backdrop, and specific disease, and not explore them further. In spending more time building Darien and helping us understand more about the Creator's affliction, it might have occupied the reader less with questions of textual authority, and more with the connection between these two worlds, as he skilfully does in the passage above. MacGregor, and perhaps Batchan, can learn from the siphonophore's collaborative existence in the dark ocean depths—they too need to find someone to rely on.

Iván Argüelles

The Eisenhower Years

it happened in the last century
when we were growing up together
there was always something going on
like getting a thousand splinters in my foot
trying to scale a rough wooden fence in long ago
may think this is absurd or the night
of the bright red asterisks and the sky a flood
of unconscious regrets bursting over the small
town lake called silver and encrustations of
fake jewelry the broad paved way with its
shops and hardware and grain-feed stores
a silo standing erect on a frozen field
waiting for the may-flies to wake up again
the agate and emerald rings you buy
in the five-and-dime joints and give away
to the next girl-friend or later almost
the time the year wouldn't turn around
trudging up the path to the big Mansion
with its pilot lights scrub oaks and pines
what was it that fretted so the ingles or
the language of disentanglement a myth of photos
broken reeds a cracked vase with paper flowers

a telephone call at the wrong hour soon it would be
mid-century pink shirts and striped ties
in the drug store with warnings about the future
lesions and bible strokes and pinball machines
the pool hall with its cigarette cadavers or
the highway that only exists on radios with loud
music big as clouds engaging the colors
of the backyard at night when the blooms
porphyry and jade learning to shine when least
expected the graduation insomnia and petrified
words that wouldn't come out a gift to be
proper and solemn head askew for the month
and rolling on lawns saturated with vodka
OK the few that survived the wreck and
the songs and polka dirges the heat especially
it would not be anything but sound
accolades in a new version of Latin the prophets
declaiming in front of the civil war cannon
and the hoosegow with its darkness a secret
whose identity could not be revealed and
so on to the next fold the minute beings
eyes and ears and the soiled pockets
money meant nothing it was all about
poetry and beauty and the large skies
that a trained eye could discern no matter
what ! when we all scattered the accident
it was because the tires couldn't stop
no one heard the rain except for the leaves
tingling with a memory of speech

05-15-21

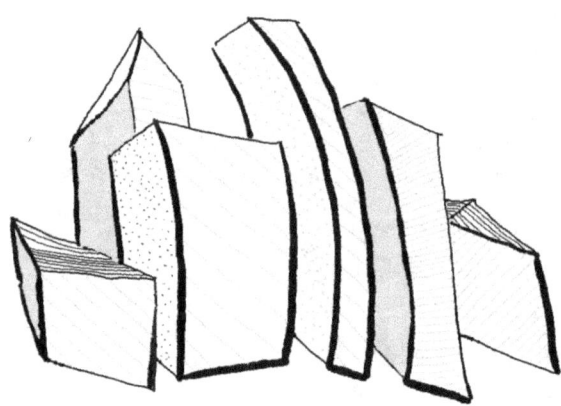

Contributors

Aaron Anstett's most recent book is *This Way to the Grand As-Is: New and Selected Poems* (Sagging Meniscus, 2020). Days, Anstett writes and edits technical documents. Nights, he expands his cooking repertoire and listens to skronky, arduous music on headphones to spare his beloved, Lesley.

Iván Argüelles is an innovative and prolific Mexican-American poet. The author of some fifty collections, he has received the William Carlos Williams Award, the American Book Award, and a Lifetime Achievement Award from the Before Columbus Foundation. A new collection, *The Blank Page*, is forthcoming from Sagging Meniscus.

Corina Bardoff is a writer and librarian currently living in New Jersey. Her fiction has appeared in *Storm Cellar*, *Menacing Hedge*, *Hysterical*, *Cream City Review*, and elsewhere.

Daniel Beauregard recently published two poetry chapbooks, *Total Darkness Means No Notifications* (Anstruther Press, 2021) and *Anatomizing Uncanny Alley* (Self Fuck, 2021), and is the co-founder of OOMPH! Press. He lives in Buenos Aires.

Jesi Bender is an artist from Upstate New York. She helms KERNPUNKT Press, a home for experimental writing. She is the author of *KINDERKRANKENHAUS* (SM, 2021) and *The Book of the Last Word* (Whiskey Tit 2019). Her shorter writing has appeared in *The Rumpus*, *Split Lip*, *Adroit Journal*, and others.

Liam Bishop is a writer from Leeds, UK. His work has appeared in *3:AM Magazine*, *Brixton Review of Books*, and *TOLKA*. He also writes fiction and essays, and interviews writers on the Rippling Pages podcast.

Kevin Boniface, an artist, writer and postman in Huddersfield, West Yorkshire, UK, is the author of *Round About Town* (Uniformbooks, 2018) and *Lost in the Post* (Old Street Publishing, 2008).

Steven Breyak is an American poet who lives with his wife and son in Osaka, Japan, where he teaches English.

Marvin Cohen is the author of many novels, plays, and collections of essays, stories, and poems. He lives on the Lower East Side of Manhattan.

David Collard is a writer, critic and researcher. A regular contributor to the *Times Literary Supplement*, the *Literary Review* and many other publications, he organizes and hosts Carthorse Orchestra, a weekly online gathering.

Elizabeth Cooperman is author (with Thomas Walton) of *The Last Mosaic* (SM, 2017) and co-editor (with David Shields) of the anthology *Life Is Short—Art Is Shorter* (Hawthorne Books, 2014). Her work has appeared in *Writer's Chronicle*, *Seattle Review*, *1913: A Journal of Forms*, and elsewhere.

Julia Drescher is the author of *Open Epic* (Delete Press, 2017).

Jack Foley's numerous books of poetry, fiction and criticism include *Visions and Affiliations*, a "chronoencyclopedia" of California poetry from 1940 to 2005, *Grief Songs* (SM, 2017) and *When Sleep Comes* (SM, 2020). He lives in Oakland and hosts a weekly radio show, *Cover to Cover*, on Berkeley's Pacifica station, KPFA.

John Patrick Higgins is a playwright, short story writer, screenwriter and director. He lives in Belfast.

Charles Holdefer is an American writer currently based in Brussels. His stories have appeared in the *New England Review*, *Chicago Quarterly Review* and *Slice*. His latest book is *Agitprop for Bedtime* (SM, 2020).

Colin James, author of *Resisting Probability* (SM, 2017), was born in the north of England near Chester. He spent most of his youth in Massachusetts before moving back to England and working as a Postman for The Royal Mail, then as a Trackman for British Rail. He met his American wife, Jane, in Chester and they currently reside in Western Massachusetts. He is a great admirer of the Scottish landscape painter John Mackenzie.

Richard Kostelanetz is an American writer, artist, critic, and editor of the avant-garde. He survives in New York, where he was born, unemployed and thus overworked.

Yahia Lababidi is an Egyptian author of nine books, including *Revolutions of the Heart* (Wipf and Stock, 2020), a book of essays and conversations exploring crises and transformation, and *Learning to Pray* (Kelsay Books, 2021) a collection of spiritual aphorisms and poems.

Kurt Luchs is the author of *Falling in the Direction of Up* (SM, 2021), *One of These Things Is Not Like the Other* (Finishing Line Press, 2019), and the humor collection *It's Funny Until Someone Loses an Eye (Then It's Really Funny)* (SM, 2017). He lives in Michigan.

Steven Moore is the author of several books and essays on modern literature, as well as the two-volume survey *The Novel: An Alternative History*. He lives in Ann Arbor, Michigan.

Kathleen Nicholls is an author and illustrator, best known for *Go Your Crohn Way*, the first of three books loosely based on her own experiences with chronic illness. She lives and works in central Scotland.

M.J. Nicholls is the author of the novels *Trimming England* (SM, 2021), *Scotland Before the Bomb* (SM, 2019), The *1002nd Book to Read Before You Die* (SM, 2018), *The Quiddity of Delusion* (SM, 2017), *The House of Writers* (SM, 2016), and *A Postmodern Belch* (2014). He lives in Glasgow.

Paolo Pergola is the author of *Passaggi—avventure di un autostoppista* (Rides: The Adventures of a Hitchhiker) (Exorma, 2013), *Attraverso la finestra di Snell* (Through Snell's Window) (Italo Svevo Edizione, 2019), and *Reset* (SM, 2021). His work has appeared in several Italian literary magazines. He is a member of OPLEPO/Opificio di Letteratura Potenziale (Workshop of Potential Literature), Italy's equivalent of France's OULIPO. He lives in Tuscany and works as a zoologist.

Dawn Raffel is the author of five books, most recently *The Strange Case of Dr. Couney: How a Mysterious European Showman Saved Thousands of American Babies*. Other books include two short story collections, a novel, and a memoir. Her stories have appeared in many magazines and anthologies, including *NOON, BOMB, Conjunctions, Exquisite Pandemic, New American Writing, The Anchor Book of New American Short Stories, Best Small Fictions*, and more.

Steven D. Schroeder's second book, *The Royal Nonesuch* (Spark Wheel Press), won the Devil's Kitchen Reading Award from Southern Illinois University. He edits the online poetry journal *$*. His poetry is available from *New England Review, Crazyhorse, Michigan Quarterly Review, The Cincinnati Review, Copper Nickel*, and *Diagram*. He works as a creative content manager for a financial marketing agency in St. Louis.

Mike Silverton's poetry appeared in the late 60s and early 70s in *Harper's, The Nation, Wormwood Review, Poetry Now, some/thing, Chelsea, Prairie Schooner, Elephant* and elsewhere. William Cole included Mike's poems in four anthologies: *Eight Lines and Under* (Macmillan, 1967), *Pith and Vinegar* (Simon and Schuster, 1969), *Poetry Brief* (Macmillan, 1971), and *Poems One Line & Longer* (Grossman, 1973).

Alina Stefanescu was born in Romania and lives in Birmingham, Alabama. Recent books include *Ribald* (Bull City Press Inch Series, Nov. 2020) and *dor*, winner of the Wandering Aengus Press Prize (July 2021). Alina's writing can be found (or is forthcoming) in journals including *Prairie Schooner, North American Review, World Literature Today, Pleiades, FLOCK, Southern Humanities Review*, and *Crab Creek Review*. She serves as Poetry Editor for *Pidgeonholes*, Poetry Editor for *Random Sample Review*, Poetry Reviewer for *Up the Staircase Quarterly*, and Co-Director of PEN America's Birmingham Chapter.

Guillermo Stitch is the author of the novella *Literature™* (2018) and the novel *Lake of Urine* (SM, 2020). He lives in Spain.

Trey Strecker teaches English at Louisiana State University in Baton Rouge.

Joe Taylor, director of Livingston Press, has published several novels and story collections, notably *Back to the Wine Jug* (SM, 2020), *Pineapple* (SM, 2017) and *The Alleged Woman: A True Tale of Ballot Intrigue* (Livingston Press, 2021).

Dan Tremaglio's stories have appeared in various publications, including *F(r)iction, Gravel, Literary Orphans*, and *Flash Fiction Magazine*, and he has twice been named a finalist for the Calvino Prize. He teaches creative writing and literature at Bellevue College outside Seattle, where he is a senior editor for the journal *Belletrist*.

Moira Walsh is a translator by day, a poet by necessity.

Thomas Walton is the author of four books: *Good Morning Bonecrusher!* (upcoming, Spuyten Duyvil), *All the Useless Things Are Mine* (SM, 2020), *The World Is All That Does Befall Us* (Ravenna Press, 2019), and, with Elizabeth Cooperman, *The Last Mosaic* (SM, 2018). He lives in Seattle, where he edits *PageBoy Magazine*.

Venetia Welby, a writer and journalist who lives in London, is the author of the novel *Mother of Darkness* (Quartet, 2017) and the forthcoming *Dreamtime* (Salt, Sept. 2021). Her essays and short fiction have appeared in *The Spectator, The London Magazine, Review 31* and the anthologies *Garden Among Fires* and *Trauma*, among others.